D1648214

Quick & Easy
GAS GRILL
COOKBOOK

BY THERMOS ®

BENJAMIN

Chief Home Economist: Betty Sullivan
Assistant Home Economist: Virginia Thompson
Editor: Phyllis Benjamin
Editorial Assistants: Susan Jablonski
    Laurie Neinfeldt, Glen Gilchrist
Design: Thomas C. Brecklin
Illustrations: Barbara Schwoegler
Typography: A-Line, Milwaukee

Copyright© 1984 Thermos A Household International Company.
All rights reserved.

Thermos
Route 75
Freeport, IL 61032

Prepared and published by: The Benjamin Company, Inc.
                          One Westchester Plaza
                          Elmsford, NY 10523

ISBN: 0-87502-132-8
Library of Congress Catalog Card Number: 84-072095
Third printing.
Printed in U.S.A.

Contents

Gas Grilling Basics

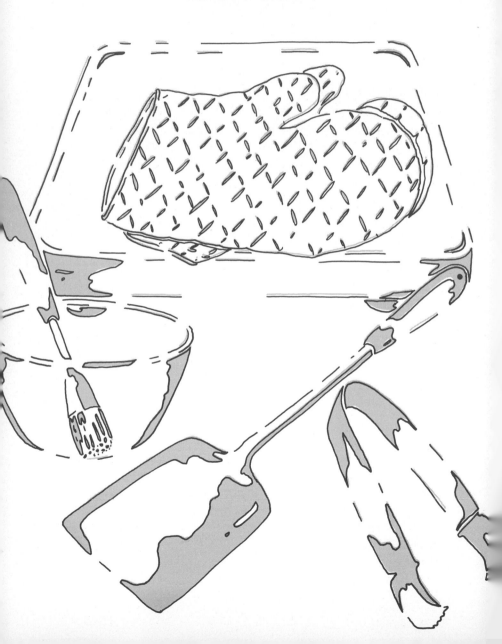

Introduction

Now you have it! All the fun and flavor of outdoor cooking are yours without the mess, unpleasant fumes, and delays of a charcoal fire. Gas grill cooking has put the emphasis on convenience for the outdoor chef. As easy to use as your microwave oven or conventional range, the gas grill is ready when you are. Whether to cook outside or inside can now be a spur of the moment decision. What's more, there's no bag of charcoal to lug, no lighter fluid to find; and, if your gas grill is equipped with an automatic ignitor, you don't even need a match! With outdoor cooking as traditional as hot dogs, apple pie, and the 4th of July, it's about time it also became an all-weather option. Now there's no reason to limit your gas grill season. Break the routine with hot-off-the-grill steak on New Year's Day. Whether you have a patio brunch for two on a bright spring day, or celebrate a family reunion at Thanksgiving with turkey and all the trimmings, you can count on your gas grill to add excitement, enticing aromas, and compliments from your guests to any meal. You'll also be pleased to know that the gas grill is just as wonderfully efficient for baking as it is for more traditional barbecuing. Homemade pies, cakes, bread, and other fresh-from-the-oven favorites are easy with your gas grill - and the kitchen stays cool. In fact, *anything* you can cook indoors can be cooked outdoors on the gas grill. Now that you have some idea of the benefits of gas grilling, let's explore the few things you need to know to quickly become an expert gas grill chef.

Assembling Your Grill

For shipping convenience and economy, all gas grills require at least some final assembly by the owner. Depending upon the model, the final assembly may require anywhere from a few minutes to a few hours. However, no complicated work or skill is really involved and your Owner's Manual has been very carefully written and fully illustrated to help you. Simply follow the step-by-step procedures and identify each part correctly and you will find assembly to be an easy and prideful accomplishment. One special tip: a muffin tray can help you keep small parts, screws, and nuts organized during the assembly process.

The Energy Source

Most gas grills use propane as their energy source. Also known as LP gas or liquefied petroleum, propane is a safe and reliable fuel. The propane tank is always shipped empty. Compressed air is used in testing the empty tank at the factory. Some of this air may remain in the tank during shipment, so don't worry if your tank appears to be "pressurized" when you remove it from the carton; any trapped air escapes quickly when you open the valve. You can rely on your propane dealer to fill your tank properly, and there is no need for you to do anything with the tank before it's filled. Use the same care in storing propane that you would for gasoline to operate the lawn mower. All petroleum-based fuels are best stored outdoors in a well-ventilated space when not in regular use. You can keep your gas grill on the patio all year long, however, by simply shutting off the gas supply at the tank. The liquefied petroleum, or propane, changes from a liquid to a gas when it comes into contact with air. Your grill is equipped with a simple device called a venturi, which is something like the carburetor in your car. It controls the amount of air that mixes with the propane to provide a gas very similar to the natural gas that may operate your conventional oven, furnace, or water heater. When you light your gas grill, the same efficient blue flame that you see on a conventional gas cooktop results.

Let's Get Cooking

The true flavor of barbecue cooking has never been provided by the charcoal. You may find that surprising, but it's true. That outdoor-cooked flavor actually comes from smoke created by the drippings off the food as it cooks. In gas grill cooking, volcanic rock or pumice is evenly distributed on the grate. The drippings hit the hot rock and the resulting smoke provides the wonderful flavor. You'll never miss that charcoal, honest! Lighting the grill is a very simple

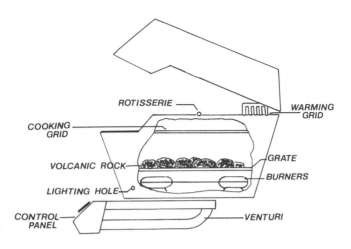

procedure. Just open the grill lid. Turn on the gas supply at the tank. Turn the control knob on the right side of the grill to HIGH. (Single burner grills have only one control knob.) Push the ignitor button. If your unit is not equipped with an automatic ignitor, insert a lighted match through the lighting hole. It is important that you do not allow excessive gas fumes to accumulate in the grill prior to ignition. After lighting the grill, most recipes call for preheating. To preheat: turn the left control knob to HIGH; then place both controls at the settings called for in the recipe. Some recipes call for preheating on HIGH and others call for preheating on MEDIUM. Preheating is required for one of two reasons: to heat the rock for most grilled food, or to preheat the oven interior for baking. It is also a self-cleaning feature of the oven, burning off any grease or residue remaining on the rock. Once the oven has preheated, you're ready to cook! As with any indoor appliance, common sense is advised for safe operation of your gas grill. Flimsy, flowing attire is not appropriate for outdoor cooking — or indoor cooking. And on very windy days, you'll want to position your grill out of the wind. It will also be helpful to realize that your gas grill is a far more efficient cooking appliance than the charcoal grill you have been using. As a result, cooking occurs much more quickly than you probably would expect. The rule to follow is, simply, be conservative. You can always return food to the grill for a few more minutes, but no one has ever found a

way to really rescue overdone food. There is nothing complicated about using your gas grill. All it takes is a little
experience and you'll be on your own. Until then, follow the
recipes and tips in this book.

Cooking Techniques

There are two basic techniques used in gas grill cooking.
Selection of the technique is simply a matter of deciding
whether you need to cook with the heat source directly
under the food (the direct method) or with the heat source
separated from the food (the indirect method). The direct
method is the choice for grilling meat, sautéing food in a
skillet, stir-fry cooking, and similar cooking procedures. You
would need to use the direct method, for example, to boil
water, fry eggs, or make pancakes. The indirect method is
selected when you want to provide a cooking environment
similar to your conventional oven. It is used for pies, cakes,
bread, casseroles, and many other dishes. It is also the best
technique for keeping food warm. To cook by the direct
method, simply place the food on the grill over an active
burner. To cook by the indirect method, place the food on the
left side of the grill with the burner on that side turned off.

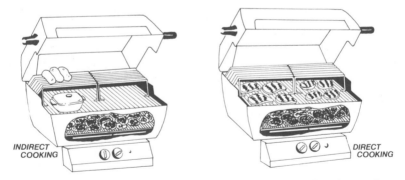

INDIRECT COOKING

DIRECT COOKING

Indirect cooking can also be done by placing food on the
warming grid. You could, for example, be cooking chicken by
the direct method on the grill surface while a vegetable
cooks by the indirect method on the warming grid. It is more
difficult to cook by the indirect method with a single-burner
grill, but it can be done. Elevate the food by placing it on a
warming rack or an inverted cast iron skillet; watch care-

fully, especially with baked goods. (Another technique for indirect cooking with a single-burner grill is to place a piece of heavy-duty aluminum foil over one half of the volcanic rocks.) Indirect cooking must be done with the lid closed.

What About Flame-Cooking?

In all meat and poultry grilling, fat drips onto the rock. Depending upon the amount of fat involved, flames can often result. Many people prefer a certain amount of flame because it provides searing for steaks, chops, hamburgers, and chicken. It's your choice. Whenever such flare-ups occur, it's up to you, the cook, to determine whether they are beneficial to the cooking process or need to be controlled. When you feel there is too much flame, simply reduce the heat and reposition the food. An alternate method, when excessive flare-up is anticipated, is to place a drip pan on the rock or to move the rock aside and place a drip pan on the grate. Cooking is then similar to the indirect method.

Smokehouse Grilling

Hickory, mesquite, applewood chips — whatever your personal favorites may be — all add to the versatility of your Structo gas grill. The tantalizing aroma and special flavor of home-smoked fish, ham, and poultry will send you off on a hunt to see "what can I try next?" Presoak wood chips according to package directions. Then form about two cups into a log (or use preformed wood chip logs, if available). Do not, however, use preformed fireplace logs because they contain petroleum products that could be dangerous to your health. Place the "log" on a piece of aluminum foil and fold foil tightly together, including the ends. Puncture 2 or 3 times with fork to let smoke out. To add moisture, move volcanic rock to the sides of the oven and position a drip pan filled with 1 or 2 inches of water on the grate. Preheat with both burners on HIGH. After 10 minutes, place wood chips in foil on rock. Turn off burner on side opposite wood chips. Place item to be smoked on cooking grid, opposite the wood chips and flame. The wood chips will smolder, creating the flavor-filled smoke. Turn remaining burner to LOW. The

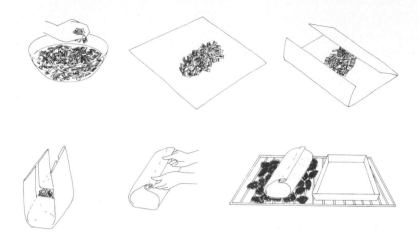

Steps in preparing wood chip package are illustrated above.

smoking process generally takes four to six hours. Don't let the timing deter you because it is well worth the wait! Check the grill once each hour and add a new foil package of wood chips if the original chips burn away. (The foil simply keeps the ashes away from the burner and speeds clean-up.)

Rotisserie Grilling

One of the most useful accessories for your gas grill is an electric rotisserie. Today, both battery-operated and electric rotisseries are available. Battery-operated rotisseries allow

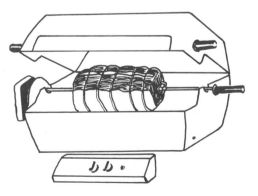

you to move away from electrical outlets and free you from extension-cord tangles. To prepare meat or poultry for rotisserie grilling, let it stand until it reaches room temperature, usually 30 to 60 minutes. This enables it to "firm up" and will permit more even cooking. Tie meat and poultry with string so that the shape is as uniform as possible. Push spit rod lengthwise through the food and fasten with fork. Check the balance and remount, if necessary, to provide consistent rotation. Position volcanic rock around side of oven and place a drip pan somewhat larger than the item being cooked on the grate. If desired, add one to two inches of water to the pan and check every 15 to 20 minutes, adding water as necessary. (Drippings, of course, can be used to make gravy later.) Let 'er roll! The preparation steps are the same for spit roasting, which only differs from rotisserie cooking in that the food is stationary. Whole fish, leg of lamb, capon, ham, and other items that are irregularly shaped may not rotate well, but they are self-basting and can be cooked on a spit.

Other Accessories

In addition to rotisseries, a wide variety of helpful accessories are available for your gas grill. They range from grill covers to special redwood shelves or barbecue utensil sets. If ever needed, replacement parts for your gas grill can also be easily obtained. A visit to your local Structo retailer should take care of all your accessory and replacement parts needs. Special assistance and ordering information can also be obtained by phoning: Structo Gas Grills (815) 232-2111.

Some Additional Tips

Throughout the recipe chapters, you'll find helpful general information as well as complete instructions for every recipe. You can also refer back to this basic chapter and these tips:

• A meat thermometer is helpful when cooking roasts and whole poultry. Follow the same procedures as for use in your conventional oven.

- When baking, don't "peek" more often than necessary. Baked goods don't like over pampering on the gas grill anymore than they do in a conventional oven.

- For extra flavor, marinate food no less than two hours before cooking. Even better, marinate overnight in the refrigerator and let food stand until it reaches room temperature before cooking.

- Let roasts and poultry stand 15 to 20 minutes before carving. This enables the juices to redistribute (they tend to accumulate just under the skin) and provides a last slice just as perfect as the first.

- To provide rare, medium, and medium-well steaks, chops, or hamburgers all in the same cooking time: select thicker portions for rare, thinner portions for medium and medium-well.

- You may find it helpful to brush the cooking grid with vegetable oil or margarine before preheating, especially if you plan to grill very lean meat.

- Many people find that they never need to clean the interior of their gas grill, aside from the cooking grid. If you have had especially heavy fat drippings, follow cooking with a "cleaning cycle." Return both burners to HIGH, close lid, and the oven will self-clean. About 15 minutes is all that is needed. A brass wire brush (steel can mar the porcelain finish) quickly cleans the cooking grid. Then, prior to preheating for the next use, turn the volcanic rock over. Any remaining residue will burn off during the preheating time.

- When selecting cookware for use with your gas grill, follow the same principles as for indoor cooking. Cookware placed directly on the grate must be suitable for stovetop cooking or broiling; cast iron, Corningware, and similar items work best (glass cannot usually be used). Cookware placed on the cooking grid need only be ovenproof or heatproof.

- Be sure to buy enough food. When the word gets around that you've got a gas grill, there's sure to be a line of neighbors at your gate!

A Break for Breakfast

Here's your chance to wake up those lazy appetites with an outdoor breakfast. Sunrise, fresh air, and your gas grill; there's no better beginning for the day. Try our Fluffy Ham Omelet (page 16), French Toast (page 18), or Swiss and Cheddar Strata (page 16) and be prepared: an outdoor breakfast will be a treat the family will look forward to often.

Bacon and Eggs au Gratin

2 tablespoons butter or margarine	6 hard-cooked eggs, coarsely chopped
1 small onion, minced	1½ cups crushed potato chips
2 tablespoons all-purpose flour	12 slices bacon, cooked crisp and crumbled
1½ cups milk	
1 cup (4 ounces) shredded Chedddar cheese	

Preheat grill on medium for 10 minutes. Butter 1½-quart baking dish; set aside. Place butter and onion in 2-quart heavy saucepan. Place on grill, close lid, and sauté 2 to 3 minutes, stirring occasionally until onion is transparent. Stir in flour. Add milk gradually. Stir through, close lid, and cook 5 to 6 minutes, stirring occasionally until sauce is smooth and has thickened. Add cheese and stir until melted; set aside. Close lid and preheat on medium for 10 minutes. Place a layer of eggs in bottom of prepared baking dish. Add half of the cheese sauce, half of the potato chips, and half of the bacon. Repeat layers. Turn off left side of grill. Turn right side to low. Place baking dish on right side of grill. Close lid and bake 7 to 10 minutes, or until heated through. Serve with toast or biscuits.

4 servings

This dish may be prepared ahead and refrigerated overnight.

Swiss and Cheddar Strata

8 slices white bread, torn
    into chunks
1½ cups (6 ounces) shredded
    Swiss cheese
1½ cups (6 ounces) shredded
    Cheddar cheese
4 eggs

2½ cups milk
2 teaspoons prepared
    mustard
3 tablespoons mayonnaise
½ teaspoon salt
⅛ teaspoon black pepper
⅛ teaspoon nutmeg

Butter bottom of 13 × 9-inch baking pan. Preheat grill on medium for 10 minutes. Meanwhile, line bottom of pan with half of the bread and top with Swiss. Add remaining bread and top with Cheddar. With heel of hand, gently press down on cheese and bread. In blender or food processor, mix eggs, milk, mustard, mayonnaise, salt, pepper, and nutmeg. Pour evenly over bread and cheese. Turn off left side of grill. Invert a baking pan over right side of grill and place strata on top. Close lid and bake 30 to 40 minutes, or until golden brown. Strata will be slightly puffed on top and set in center. Cut into large squares and serve.

12 servings

Fluffy Ham Omelet

5 eggs, separated
1 cup dairy sour cream,
    divided
⅛ teaspoon white pepper

½ teaspoon dry mustard
1 cup minced cooked ham
2 tablespoons butter or
    margarine

Preheat grill on medium for 10 minutes. Beat egg whites in small bowl with electric mixer until stiff; set aside. Beat yolks in large bowl until lemon colored and slightly thickened. Blend in ½ cup sour cream, pepper, and mustard. Gently fold in egg whites and ham. Place 10-inch skillet on grill. Add butter and cook until butter is melted. Pour egg mixture into skillet. Close lid and cook 5 minutes or until omelet is lightly browned on bottom. Turn off left side of grill and place inverted baking pan on left side of grill. Place skillet on baking pan. Close lid and bake 10 to 15 minutes, or until golden brown. Loosen omelet with spatula and slide onto warm serving plate. Spread with remaining sour cream.

2 to 3 servings

TIMING GUIDE FOR COOKING EGGS

Style	Amount	Lid Position	Grill Setting	Approx. Total Cooking Time
Fried	4-6	Open	High	1-2 minutes
Scrambled	2-3	Open	Medium	1-2 minutes
	4-6	Open	Medium	3-5 minutes
Baked	3-4	Closed	High	7-10 minutes
Poached	1-4	Closed	High	Boil 2 cups water in skillet for 7-10 minutes
				Eggs 2-4 minutes

Bread 'n Eggs Parmesan

6 eggs
2 tablespoons cream or
    half and half
¼ teaspoon salt
    Dash pepper
4 tablespoons butter or
    margarine

2 slices white bread,
    cut in ¼-inch cubes
2 tablespoons Parmesan
    cheese

Beat eggs, cream, salt, and pepper in medium bowl; set aside. Remove cooking grid from grill. Move volcanic rock to one side. Place large skillet on grate. Arrange rock around skillet. Add butter to skillet and cook on medium until melted. Add bread cubes and stir to coat with butter. Cook until lightly browned on all sides, about 6 minutes. Reduce heat to low. Pour egg mixture over bread cubes. Stir lightly with a spatula using a turning motion until eggs are set. Sprinkle with Parmesan cheese and serve.

4 servings

French Toast

2 eggs, lightly beaten
⅔ cup milk
1 tablespoon brown sugar
½ teaspoon salt

3 to 4 tablespoons butter
   or margarine, divided
8 slices French, white, or
   whole wheat bread

Combine eggs, milk, brown sugar, and salt in shallow dish. Stir until sugar is dissolved; set aside. Remove cooking grid and place volcanic rock on left side of grate. Place heavy skillet on right side of grate and surround with volcanic rock. Add 1 tablespoon butter to skillet and cook on low until butter is melted. Dip bread, one slice at a time, into egg mixture, turning to coat both sides. As each slice is coated, place bread in hot skillet and cook until both sides are brown, turning once with a spatula. Add butter as needed to keep slices from sticking. Place toast in serving platter as each piece is finished and keep warm. Serve with butter, maple syrup, honey, jam, applesauce, or confectioners sugar.

Alternate Method: Preheat grill on medium for 10 minutes. Place skillet or griddle on grill. Add butter and dipped bread as above. Close lid. Cook 3 minutes. Turn bread slices over and cook another 2 to 3 minutes or until brown. With this method, you can use the other side of the grill for sausage or bacon.

4 servings

You can substitute ⅔ cup orange juice for milk and add 1 teaspoon cinnamon to egg mixture for Orange-Cinnamon French Toast.

Canadian Bacon and Shirred Eggs

8 slices (8 ounces)
   Canadian bacon
¼ cup cream or
   half and half

4 large eggs
Pepper and paprika
1 tablespoon chopped
   parsley

Preheat grill on medium for 10 minutes. Brown Canadian bacon in skillet on grill. Butter four ramekins or custard cups. Arrange two slices of bacon in each. Add 1 tablespoon cream. Break egg carefully into each ramekin. Sprinkle with pepper and paprika. Turn off left side of grill. Place ramekins on right side of grill, close lid, and bake 10 to 15 minutes, or until desired doneness. Sprinkle with parsley and serve hot.

4 servings

Pork Sausage and Scrambled Eggs

6 eggs	3 tablespoons butter or
½ cup dairy sour cream	margarine, melted
½ teaspoon salt	8 to 10 precooked pork
⅛ teaspoon cayenne	sausage links
	(8 ounces)

Preheat grill on medium for 10 minutes. Butter 10-inch skillet; set aside. Combine eggs, sour cream, salt, cayenne, and butter in medium bowl. Pour into prepared skillet. Place skillet on right side of grill. Place sausages on left side of grill. Cook with lid closed 5 to 8 minutes, or until eggs reach desired doneness and sausages have browned. Turn sausages and stir eggs frequently.

3 servings

Rancho Grande Eggs

5 eggs	1 can (4 ounces) mild
2 cups (8 ounces) shredded	green chilies,
Monterey Jack cheese	chopped
1 cup ricotta cheese	½ teaspoon baking powder
¼ cup all-purpose flour	1 teaspoon paprika

Preheat grill on medium for 10 minutes. Butter a 10-inch baking dish; set aside. Beat eggs in large bowl until frothy. Whisk in remaining ingredients, except paprika, until blended. Pour into prepared dish. Sprinkle with paprika. Turn off left side of grill. Place dish on left side of grill, close lid, and bake 25 to 30 minutes, or until set in center. Serve warm.

4 servings

Peach Breakfast Squares

3 cups biscuit mix
1 cup all-purpose flour
1 cup lightly packed
   brown sugar
¾ cup butter or margarine
1 can (29 ounces) cling
   peach slices, drained

6 egg yolks
3 tablespoons sugar
6 tablespoons cream
½ teaspoon nutmeg

Butter 15 × 10-inch jelly roll pan; set aside. Prepare dough from biscuit mix according to package directions. Spread dough over bottom and slightly up sides of prepared pan. Preheat grill on medium for 10 minutes. Combine flour and brown sugar in medium bowl. With two knives or pastry blender, cut in butter. Spoon evenly over biscuit dough. Arrange peach slices in rows over brown sugar mixture. Turn off left side of grill. Invert baking pan over left side of grill. Place peach dish on inverted pan. Close lid and bake 20 to 25 minutes, or until crust is lightly browned. Meanwhile, beat egg yolks, sugar, cream, and nutmeg. Pour evenly over peaches. Close lid and bake 10 to 12 minutes, or until custard is set. Cut in squares and serve.

24 servings

Orange French Toast

2 eggs, lightly beaten
1 cup orange juice
10 slices raisin bread

1½ cups vanilla wafer or
   graham cracker crumbs
Butter or margarine

Preheat right side of grill on high for 5 minutes, then turn to medium. Season griddle or large skillet with vegetable oil. Place griddle on right cooking grid and heat 5 minutes. Combine eggs and orange juice in shallow pan. Melt 1 tablespoon butter on griddle. Quickly dip bread into egg mixture, then coat both sides with crumbs. Fry bread 1 to 2 minutes on each side, or until browned, adding butter as needed.

5 servings

Cornmeal Griddle Cakes

1 cup all-purpose flour	2 eggs, lightly beaten
1 cup cornmeal	2 cups milk
1 tablespoon baking powder	1 tablespoon molasses or corn syrup
½ teaspoon salt	Butter or margarine

Preheat grill on medium for 10 minutes. Combine dry ingredients in large bowl; set aside. Combine eggs, milk, and molasses; add to dry ingredients and stir until blended. Place skillet or griddle on grill. Add 1 tablespoon butter and cook until melted. Pour about 3 tablespoonfuls of batter for each pancake. Close lid and cook about 1½ minutes. Turn cakes over with pancake turner to brown other side. Repeat with remaining batter. Add butter as necessary to keep batter from sticking. Serve warm with butter.

18 to 20 pancakes

Grill-Top Pancakes

1½ cups all-purpose flour	3 tablespoons butter, melted
3 tablespoons sugar	1 large egg, lightly beaten
1 teaspoon baking powder	
½ teaspoon baking soda	
½ teaspoon salt	Maple syrup or fruit preserves
1¼ cups milk	

Combine all ingredients, except syrup in mixing bowl; stir until ingredients are just moistened. Do not overmix. Preheat right side of grill on high for 5 minutes, then turn to medium-high. Season griddle or large skillet with vegetable oil. Place griddle on right cooking grid and heat 5 minutes. Cook batter for 1 to 2 minutes, or until tops are bubbly. Turn and cook until browned. Repeat with remaining batter. Serve with maple syrup or fruit preserves.

6 servings

Patio Party
Partners

Whether it's just Mom, Dad, and the kids or a no-holds-barred party, these meal startoffs set the mood for fun and enjoyment. Lip-smacking Dogs 'n Things (page 30) and Tuna Chowder (page 25) appeal to the young set. Green Chili Snacks (page 30) and hearty Cheese 'n Ale Soup (page 23) are party-pro specials. All these and more set the mood for a gathering with gusto.

Cheese 'n Ale Soup

3 tablespoons butter or margarine
1 small onion, chopped
1 carrot, shredded
1 stalk celery, minced
3 tablespoons all-purpose flour
¼ teaspoon freshly ground pepper

2 cups milk
⅓ cup water
1 teaspoon instant chicken bouillon granules
1 jar (8 ounces) process cheese spread
1 cup beer

Combine butter, onion, carrot, and celery in 2-quart casserole; set aside. Remove cooking grid from grill. Move volcanic rock to one side of grill. Place casserole on grate. Cook on high, with lid open, about 5 minutes, or until vegetables are tender. Stir in flour and pepper. Stir in milk, water, and bouillon granules. Cook and stir until thickened. Add cheese and stir until melted. Stir in beer. Heat through but do not boil.

4 servings

Minty Scallops

¾ cup vegetable oil
1 tablespoon vinegar
2 tablespoons finely
  chopped fresh mint
1 teaspoon salt
1 teaspoon basil

1 clove garlic, minced
¼ teaspoon freshly ground
  pepper
⅛ teaspoon hot pepper
  sauce
2 pounds sea scallops

Combine all ingredients except scallops in large bowl. Add scallops and stir lightly to coat. Cover and refrigerate 3 to 4 hours. Drain scallops, reserving marinade. Thread scallops onto metal skewers; set aside. Lightly grease right side of cooking grid. Preheat grill on medium for 10 minutes, then turn left side of grill off. Place skewers on right side of cooking grid and brush with marinade. Close lid; grill 4 to 6 minutes, or until scallops are opaque, turning and basting twice. Remove from skewers and transfer to serving bowl. Serve with wooden picks.

12 to 16 servings

Fish Chowder

4 slices bacon, cut in
  pieces
3 medium onions, sliced
1½ pounds haddock
5 medium potatoes, peeled
  and diced
3 cups hot water
2 teaspoons salt

¼ teaspoon white pepper
4 cups milk
1 can (12 ounces)
  evaporated milk
1 tablespoon butter or
  margarine
Nutmeg
Soup crackers

Place bacon in 6-quart kettle. Remove cooking grid from grill. Move volcanic rock to one side of grill. Place kettle on grate. Cook bacon over medium heat, with lid open, until crisp. Remove from pan with slotted spoon and drain on paper towels. Add onions to bacon drippings. Cook, stirring often, until onions are golden. Add fish, potatoes, water, salt, and pepper. Cover kettle and turn heat to low. Close lid and cook 20 to 25 minutes, or until potatoes are tender. Add milk, evaporated milk, and butter. Sprinkle with bacon and nutmeg. Ladle into soup bowls and serve with crackers.

6 to 8 servings

Tuna Corn Chowder

2 cans (9¼ ounces each)
tuna, packed in oil
4 medium onions, sliced
5 medium potatoes, peeled
and thinly sliced
2 teaspoons salt
⅛ teaspoon freshly ground
pepper

3 cups water
4 cups milk
1 package (10 ounces)
frozen whole kernel
corn
2 tablespoons butter or
margarine

Drain oil from tuna into 6-quart kettle; set tuna aside. Add onions.
Remove cooking grid from grill. Move volcanic rock to one side of
grill. Place kettle on grate. Cook onions over medium heat, with lid
open, stirring until golden. Add potatoes, salt, pepper, and water.
Cover kettle and turn heat to low. Close lid; cook 15 to 20 minutes,
or until potatoes are tender. Stir in milk, corn, and tuna; cover
kettle. Close lid and cook 15 to 20 minutes or until heated through.
Float butter on top of chowder and serve.

6 to 8 servings

Shrimp Italiano

½ cup olive oil
2 tablespoons lemon juice
1 teaspoon oregano
2 cloves garlic, minced
½ teaspoon salt

⅛ teaspoon freshly ground
pepper
2 pounds large shrimp,
shelled and deveined

Combine all ingredients except shrimp in bowl large enough to
hold shrimp. Add shrimp and stir lightly to coat. Cover and refrigerate 3 to 4 hours. Drain shrimp from marinade, reserving marinade. Thread shrimp onto metal skewers; set aside. Lightly grease
right side of cooking grid. Preheat grill on medium for 10 minutes,
then turn left side off. Place skewers on right side of cooking grid
and brush with marinade. Close lid; grill 6 to 8 minutes, or until
shrimp is opaque and firm, basting once during cooking time.
Remove from skewers and transfer to serving bowl. Serve with
any remaining marinade on the side.

12 to 16 servings

Polynesian Shrimp Kabobs

⅓ cup soy sauce
⅓ cup white wine
1 teaspoon freshly ground pepper
½ teaspoon ground ginger

2 pounds large shrimp, shelled and deveined
1 can (5¼ ounces) pineapple chunks

Combine soy sauce, wine, pepper, and ginger in bowl large enough to hold shrimp. Add shrimp and stir lightly to coat. Cover and refrigerate 3 to 4 hours. Drain shrimp, reserving marinade. Thread shrimp and pineapple alternately onto metal skewers and baste with marinade; set aside. Lightly grease right side of cooking grid. Preheat grill on medium for 10 minutes, then turn left side off. Place skewers on right side of cooking grid and baste with marinade. Close lid and grill 6 to 8 minutes, or until shrimp are opaque and firm, basting with marinade once during cooking time. Remove from skewers to serving platter. Serve with wooden picks.

Variations: Omit marinade ingredients above. Alternate shrimp, cherry tomatoes, and small whole onions on skewers. Brush with olive oil; grill as above. Before skewering shrimp, roll each in a bacon strip. Baste with marinade; grill as above.

Slit shrimp partially through centers without cutting completely. Stuff with anchovies and wrap in a bacon slice. Brush with marinade; grill as above.

Alternate shrimp with green pepper chunks and onion slices. Brush with marinade; grill as above.

12 to 16 servings

Hot Buttered Brie

1 wheel (16 ounces) Brie cheese, well ripened
¼ cup butter, softened

1 cup slivered almonds, lightly toasted

Place cheese in au gratin dish just large enough to hold it. Spread top with butter and sprinkle with nuts. Cover and set aside. Preheat grill on medium for 10 minutes, then turn left side of grill off and right side to low. Invert a pan on left side of cooking grid. Place dish on inverted pan. Close lid and bake about 10 minutes, or until cheese is soft and creamy. Serve with assorted crackers.

8 to 10 servings

Grilled Rumaki

18 slices bacon
¼ cup soy sauce
¼ teaspoon garlic powder
½ pound chicken livers,
    rinsed, drained, and
    cut in 1-inch pieces

1 can (8 ounces) sliced
    water chestnuts,
    drained

Cook bacon in large skillet until almost done, but not crisp; drain fat. Cut bacon slices in half. Combine soy sauce and garlic powder in small bowl. Dip livers in sauce. Wrap 1 piece liver and 1 slice water chestnut in 1 piece bacon. Secure with wooden picks. Place in a rotisserie basket. Preheat grill on medium for 10 minutes, then turn to low. Insert spit rod through basket. Attach spit rod to rotisserie motor and start motor. Close lid; grill 5 minutes, or until bacon is crisp and liver is done.

about 36 appetizers

If not using rotisserie grill basket, line cooking grid with lightly greased heavy-duty aluminum foil. Place rumaki on foil and grill 6 to 8 minutes, turning after 4 minutes.

Barbecued Chicken Wings

2 to 3 pounds chicken
    wings
1 cup soy sauce
¼ cup white wine

1 tablespoon sugar
2 cloves garlic, crushed
1 teaspoon ginger
⅛ teaspoon cayenne pepper

Cut chicken wings into 3 pieces at joints; discard wing tips. Combine all ingredients, except chicken wings, in a double plastic bag. Add chicken wings. Seal bag and refrigerate at least 8 hours, turning occasionally. Grease cooking grid lightly. Preheat grill on medium for 10 minutes, then turn to medium-low. Drain wings from marinade; reserve marinade. Place wings on cooking grid. Close lid; grill 10 to 15 minutes, or until chicken is no longer pink near bone, turning and basting once with marinade.

12 servings

Cocktail Burger Balls

½ cup French onion dip
3 tablespoons bread
   crumbs
¼ teaspoon salt
   Dash freshly ground
   pepper
1 pound lean ground beef

⅓ cup catsup
2 tablespoons prepared
   mustard
1 teaspoon Worcestershire
   sauce
½ teaspoon prepared
   horseradish

Combine dip, bread crumbs, salt, and pepper in large bowl; blend well. Add ground beef; blend well. Shape into walnut-size balls. Cover and refrigerate. Preheat grill on high for 10 minutes, then turn left side of grill off and right side to low. Line heated cooking grid with heavy-duty aluminum foil. Turn edges of foil up. Arrange meatballs on foil. Close lid; grill 20 to 25 minutes or until well browned on all sides lifting corners of foil to turn meatballs during cooking. Transfer to serving bowl. Combine catsup, mustard, Worcestershire, and horseradish. Serve meatballs with wooden picks, dipped in sauce.

16 to 18 meatballs

Beef Teriyaki Appetizers

1 cup dry sherry
1 cup soy sauce
3 tablespoons brown sugar
1 tablespoon minced fresh
   ginger

2 cloves garlic, minced
2 pounds beef rump roast,
   sirloin tip, or
   tenderloin, cut in
   1½-inch chunks

Preheat grill on medium for 10 minutes. Combine all ingredients, except meat, in small bowl. Thread meat chunks onto metal skewers. Brush with marinade. Place skewers in wire grill basket. Place on cooking grid. Close lid; grill 4 minutes. Turn basket, baste with marinade, and grill another 4 minutes. Remove from skewers and serve with wooden picks.

about 35 appetizers

Sausage and Cheese Finger Sandwiches

1½ pounds Monterey Jack
cheese, sliced
1 cup (4 ounces) shredded
mozzarella cheese
1 pound mild Italian
sausage, parboiled

1 loaf (1 pound) French
bread, thinly sliced,
or 6 French rolls, sliced

Arrange Monterey Jack slices in shallow metal pan. Sprinkle mozzarella on top; set aside. Lightly grease right side of cooking grid. Preheat grill on medium for 10 minutes. Turn left side of grill off. Place sausage on right side of cooking grid and pan with cheese on left side of cooking grid. Close lid and grill about 6 minutes, turning sausage often, until well browned on all sides. Stir cheese occasionally. Remove cheese and sausage from grill. Slice sausage. Invite guests to make small sandwiches of French bread topped with melted cheese and a slice of sausage.

6 to 8 servings

To parboil sausage: pierce sausage and place in microwave-safe baking dish. Cover with plastic wrap. Microcook on High 4 to 6 minutes or until sausage loses its pink color.

Sausage Cheese Balls

1 pound bulk pork sausage
2½ cups (10 ounces) sharp
Cheddar cheese, grated
3 cups buttermilk baking
mix

2 tablespoons minced
onion

Combine all ingredients in large bowl; blend well. Shape into 1-inch balls. Preheat grill on high for 10 minutes, then turn to medium-low. Line cooking grid with 18-inch square of heavy-duty aluminum foil. Turn edges of foil up. Arrange meatballs on foil. Close lid and grill until well browned on all sides, lifting corners of foil to turn meatballs during cooking.

6 servings

Green Chili Snacks

1 package (3 ounces)
   cream cheese,
   softened
½ cup (2 ounces) shredded
   Cheddar cheese
3 to 4 tablespoons chopped
   mild or hot green
   chilies, drained

2 tablespoons minced onion
5 drops hot pepper sauce
1 can (8 ounces)
   refrigerated crescent
   rolls

Combine all ingredients except rolls in small bowl; blend well. Separate crescent dough into 4 rectangles; press perforations to seal dough. Spread ¼ of the cheese mixture over each rectangle. Roll up, jelly-roll fashion, starting from long side. Cut each roll into 10 slices. Place slices on greased baking sheet. Cover and place in refrigerator. Preheat grill on medium for 10 minutes, then turn left side of the grill off. Invert a baking pan on right cooking grid. Remove baking sheet from refrigerator and place in grill on inverted pan. Close lid; grill 12 to 15 minutes, or until snack rolls are golden brown, rotating baking sheet after 6 minutes.

40 snacks

Dogs 'n Things

⅓ cup prepared mustard
½ cup currant jelly
2 packages (8 ounces each)
   cocktail brown-and-serve
   sausages, cut in
   bite-size pieces

Preheat right side of grill on medium for 10 minutes. Combine mustard and jelly in metal saucepan and place on right side of cooking grid. Heat until jelly melts, stirring often. Add sausages to jelly mixture; cook 10 to 12 minutes, or until sausages are heated through. Serve with wooden picks from pan or transfer to heated serving dish.

Variation: Substitute 1 pound hot dogs for cocktail sausages, apricot preserves for currant jelly, and ¼ cup horseradish mustard for prepared mustard.

about 40 appetizers

Chili Bean Dip

1 can (1 pound 12 ounces)
   pork and
   beans in tomato sauce
½ medium onion, quartered
1 to 2 tablespoons
   chili powder

1 teaspoon cumin
¼ teaspoon garlic powder
⅛ teaspoon cayenne pepper
6 drops hot pepper sauce
1 bag (16 ounces) large
   corn chips

Combine pork and beans and onion in blender or food processor; blend until smooth. Blend in remaining ingredients, except corn chips, and turn into 1½-quart casserole. Remove cooking grid from grill. Move volcanic rock to one side. Place casserole on grate. Arrange rock around casserole. Bring mixture to a boil over low heat, with lid open, stirring often. Remove from grill and serve with corn chips.

2 cups

Hot and Spicy Slim Jims

¼ cup butter or margarine,
   melted
1 teaspoon Worcestershire
   sauce
⅛ teaspoon hot pepper
   sauce

½ teaspoon garlic powder
⅛ teaspoon paprika
1 package (4½ ounces)
   plain bread sticks
2 tablespoons grated
   Parmesan cheese

Combine butter, Worcestershire, hot pepper sauce, garlic powder, and paprika in small bowl. Brush butter mixture over bread sticks and top with cheese. Wrap bread sticks in double thickness of heavy-duty aluminum foil. Shake packet to distribute cheese. Pre-heat grill on medium for 10 minutes, then turn left side of grill off. Place packet on right side of cooking grid. Grill, with lid open, 6 to 8 minutes, turning often. Serve hot.

3 to 4 servings

All-American Beef

You'll never have beef any better than on your versatile gas grill. Steaks, roasts, burgers - you might find that you've retired your conventional oven and broiler for good. There's just no substitute for the flavor of grilled beef. Casseroles, too, are quick and easy outdoors, in any weather.

Super Easy Steak

1 beef porterhouse, sirloin tip, or top round steak (about 3 pounds), or 4 to 6 beef T-bone or New York strip steaks (10 to 14 ounces each)	Beef Seasoning Salt (page 111)

Trim fat from steak. Slash edges every 1½ inches to prevent steak from curling. Lightly grease cooking grid. Preheat grill on medium for 10 minutes. Place large steak in center of cooking grid; place single steaks about 2 inches apart. Close lid and grill large steak 7 to 10 minutes on each side (rare), or until desired doneness; grill single steaks 5 to 8 minutes. If flare-ups occur, rearrange steaks on cooking grid. Transfer large steak to cutting board and cut into thin slices. Season all steaks with Beef Seasoning Salt.

6 to 8 servings

Curried Beef Kabobs

½ cup olive or vegetable oil	3 cloves garlic, minced
½ cup lemon juice	3 pounds boneless beef, cut in 1½-inch cubes
1 to 2 tablespoons curry powder	Hot cooked rice

Combine oil, lemon juice, curry powder, and garlic in bowl large enough to hold beef. Add beef and stir to coat. Cover and refrigerate at least 2 hours, turning occasionally. Drain beef, reserving marinade. Thread beef onto metal skewers. Lightly grease cooking grid. Preheat grill on medium for 10 minutes, then turn left side of grill off. Place skewers on right cooking grid and brush with marinade. Close lid and grill 18 to 21 minutes, turning and basting often. Serve with rice.

6 servings

Steak and Cheese

⅓ cup dry red wine	1 beef flank steak
3 tablespoons vegetable oil	(about 1½ pounds)
¼ teaspoon thyme	6 English muffins,
¼ teaspoon marjoram	split and buttered
1 clove garlic, minced	6 large slices Muenster or
¼ cup chopped onion	Swiss cheese
1 bay leaf	Minced green onions

Combine wine, oil, thyme, marjoram, garlic, onion, and bay leaf in small bowl; blend well. Pour over steak in plastic bag or shallow pan. Seal bag or cover pan. Refrigerate at least 4 hours, turning occasionally. Lightly grease right side of cooking grid. Preheat grill on medium for 10 minutes, then turn left side of grill off. Drain steak, discarding marinade. Place steak on left cooking grid. Close lid and grill 5 minutes. Turn steak and place muffins, buttered side down, on right cooking grid to toast. Grill 5 more minutes, or until desired doneness. Transfer steak to cutting board and cut into thin diagonal slices. Cut cheese slices in half and lay one half-slice on each muffin half. Sprinkle with green onions. Top with steak slices and serve.

6 servings

Pepper-Crusted Steak

1 boneless beef sirloin	⅓ cup cracked
steak (3 to 4 pounds)	peppercorns
2 tablespoons vegetable oil	Sliced rye bread, toasted
⅓ cup coarse salt	(optional)

Trim fat from steak. Slash edges every 1½ inches to prevent steak from curling. Brush oil on both sides of steak. Rub with salt and pepper; set aside. Lightly grease right side of cooking grid. Preheat grill on medium for 10 minutes, then turn left side of grill off and right side to medium-low. Place steak on right cooking grid. Close lid and grill 20 minutes, or until desired doneness, turning after 10 minutes. If flare-ups occur, move steak to left cooking grid. Transfer to cutting board, brush off some of the salt and pepper, and cut into thin diagonal slices. Serve on toasted rye bread, if desired.

6 servings

TIMING GUIDE FOR COOKING BEEF
Lid Closed

Cut	Size/ Weight	Doneness	Grill Setting	Approx. Total Cooking Time
Brisket	3 pounds	Rare (140°F)	Low	2-2½ hours
		Medium (160°F)	Low	2½-3 hours
		Well Done (170°F)	Low	3½-4 hours
	5 pounds	Rare (140°F)	Low	3-4½ hours
		Medium (160°F)	Low	4½-5 hours
		Well Done (170°F)	Low	5½-6 hours
Hamburgers	¼ pound	Rare	Medium	7-9 minutes
	½ inch thick	Medium	Medium	9-11 minutes
		Well Done	Medium	11-14 minutes
Kabobs	1½ inch cubes	Rare	Medium	5 minutes
		Medium	Medium	8 minutes
		Well Done	Medium	10 minutes
Roasts				
Standing Rib	5 pounds	Rare (140°F)	Low	1½-2 hours
		Medium (160°F)	Low	2-3 hours
		Well Done (170°F)	Low	2-3 hours
Rolled Rib (Rotisserie)	5 pounds	Rare (140°F)	Low	1½-2½ hours
		Medium (160°F)	Low	2-3 hours
		Well Done (170°F)	Low	3½ hours
Rump; Sirloin Tip; Top Round	3 pounds	Rare (140°F)	Low	50-60 minutes
		Medium (160°F)	Low	1-1½ hours
		Well Done (170°F)	Low	1½-2 hours
	5 pounds	Rare (140°F)	Low	60-90 minutes
		Medium (160°F)	Low	1½-2 hours
		Well Done (170°F)	Low	2-2½ hours
Tenderloin	2-3 pounds	Rare (140°F)	Medium	25-30 minutes
	4-6 pounds	Rare (140°F)	Medium	35-40 minutes

TIMING GUIDE FOR COOKING BEEF
(Continued)
Lid Closed

Cut	Size/ Weight	Doneness	Grill Setting	Approx. Total Cooking Time
Steaks				
Chuck	1 inch	Rare	Med. high	20-25 minutes
	thick	Medium	Med. high	25-30 minutes
		Well Done	Med. high	30-35 minutes
Rib; Delmonico	1 inch	Rare	Med. low	5-6 minutes
	thick	Medium	Med. low	6-8 minutes
		Well Done	Med. low	8-10 minutes
	1½ inches	Rare	Med. low	10-15 minutes
	thick	Medium	Med. low	15-20 minutes
		Well Done	Med. low	20-25 minutes
Sirloin;	1 inch	Rare	Med. low	5-6 minutes
Porterhouse	thick	Medium	Med. low	6-8 minutes
		Well Done	Med. low	8-10 minutes
	1½ inches	Rare	Med. low	10-15 minutes
	thick	Medium	Med. low	15-20 minutes
		Well Done	Med. low	20-25 minutes
	2 inches	Rare	Med. low	14-20 minutes
	thick	Medium	Med. low	20-25 minutes
		Well Done	Med. low	25-30 minutes
Tenderloin	¼-½ pounds	Rare	Medium	3-5 minutes
(Filet Mignon)		Medium	Medium	5-8 minutes

Open-face
Steak and Mushroom Sandwich

½ cup red wine
2 tablespoons lemon juice
¼ cup olive or vegetable oil
1 teaspoon Worcestershire
   sauce
½ cup chopped onion
1 clove garlic, minced
½ teaspoon salt
⅛ teaspoon freshly ground
   pepper

1½ pounds beef top
   sirloin steak, trimmed
1 pound fresh mushrooms,
   sliced
6 tablespoons butter or
   margarine
6 slices light rye bread,
   buttered
Chopped parsley

Combine wine, lemon juice, oil, Worcestershire, onion, garlic, salt, and pepper in small bowl; blend well. Pour over steak in plastic bag or shallow dish. Seal bag or cover dish. Refrigerate at least 2 hours, turning steak occasionally. Sauté mushrooms in butter about 5 minutes, or until tender; set aside. Lightly grease right cooking grid. Preheat grill on medium for 10 minutes, then turn left side of grill off. Drain steak, reserving marinade. Place steak on right cooking grid. Place mushrooms in pan on left cooking grid to keep warm. Close lid and grill about 8 minutes, basting once. Turn steak; place bread buttered side down, around edge of grill. Grill 8 minutes, checking bread often to avoid burning. Remove steak to platter and cut into thin slices. Place 3 or 4 steak slices on each piece of bread and top with mushrooms. Sprinkle with parsley and serve.

6 servings

Beef Tenderloin in Garlic Marinade

1 beef tenderloin (3 pounds)	4 cloves garlic, minced
½ cup soy sauce	1 teaspoon hot pepper sauce
½ cup red wine	Dash freshly ground pepper
¼ cup olive or vegetable oil	

Place beef in shallow dish. Combine remaining ingredients and pour over beef. Cover and refrigerate 24 hours, turning occasionally. Drain beef, reserving marinade. Lightly grease right side of cooking grid. Preheat grill on high for 1 minute, then turn left side of grill off and right side to medium. Place beef on right cooking grid. Close lid and grill 25 minutes, turning once and basting occasionally, until desired doneness. Remove to serving platter and let stand 10 minutes before slicing.

6 servings

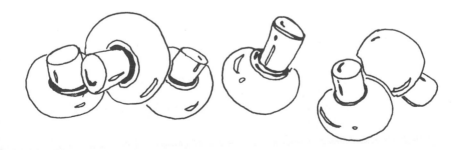

Veal and Vegetable Kabobs

½ cup dry white wine
5 tablespoons vegetable oil
¼ cup catsup
½ teaspoon basil
½ teaspoon salt
⅛ teaspoon freshly ground
pepper

1 pound boneless veal,
cut in 1-inch cubes
2 green peppers, cut in
1- inch cubes
12 large mushroom caps
12 firm cherry tomatoes

Combine wine, oil, catsup, basil, salt, and pepper in bowl just large enough to hold veal. Add veal and stir to coat. Cover and refrigerate at least 1 hour, stirring once. Drain veal, reserving marinade. Thread veal onto 2 metal skewers; thread green peppers, mushrooms, and tomatoes onto separate skewers. Lightly grease cooking grid. Preheat grill on medium for 10 minutes, then turn to low. Place skewers with veal on cooking grid. Close lid and grill 6 minutes; turn. Place skewers with green peppers, mushrooms, and tomatoes on cooking grid. Close lid and grill 3 minutes. Brush all kabobs with marinade and grill 3 minutes, or until veal is tender and vegetables are tender-crisp. Brush with marinade and serve.

4 servings

Veal Cutlets

2 pounds veal cutlets
(¼ inch thick)
¼ cup lemon juice
1 tablespoon minced green
onion
2 tablespoons chopped
parsley

1 clove garlic, pressed
⅓ cup vegetable oil
½ teaspoon salt
⅛ teaspoon freshly ground
pepper

Pound cutlets between sheets of waxed paper to ⅛-inch thickness. Place in shallow pan. Combine remaining ingredients and pour over veal. Cover and refrigerate at least 2 hours, turning occasionally. Lightly grease cooking grid. Preheat grill on medium for 10 minutes, then turn to low. Drain veal, reserving marinade. Place veal on cooking grid. Close lid and grill 8 to 10 minutes, turning once and basting with marinade.

4 to 6 servings

Beef and Vegetable Kabobs

1 cup dry red wine
½ cup soy sauce
½ cup olive or vegetable oil
1 clove garlic, minced
2 pounds boneless beef
    top round, cut in
    1½-inch cubes

12 new potatoes, cooked
12 firm cherry tomatoes
2 green peppers,
    cut in 1½-inch chunks

Combine wine, soy sauce, oil, and garlic in bowl large enough to hold beef. Add beef and stir to coat. Cover and refrigerate at least 2 hours, stirring occasionally. Drain beef, reserving marinade. Thread beef onto metal skewers. Lightly grease right side of cooking grid. Preheat grill on medium for 10 minutes, then turn left side of grill off. Place skewers on right cooking grid. Close lid; grill 18 to 21 minutes, turning and basting often. Thread potatoes, tomatoes, and green peppers onto metal skewers and brush with marinade. Place on outside edge of cooking grid during last 15 minutes of cooking time, turning and basting once.

4 servings

Tex-Mex Chili

2 tablespoons vegetable oil
2 pounds lean ground beef
2 cups chopped onions
3 cans (16 ounces each) red
    kidney beans, drained
1 can (1 pound 12 ounces)
    tomatoes

1 can (6 ounces) chopped
    green chilies, drained
½ cup beef broth
3 to 4 tablespoons
    chili powder
2 teaspoons cumin
1 clove garlic, minced

Combine oil, beef, and onions in 6-quart kettle. Remove cooking grid from grill. Move volcanic rock to one side. Place kettle on grate. Arrange rock around kettle. Cook on high, stirring frequently to break up meat, until beef is no longer pink and onions are tender. Add remaining ingredients; stir to break up tomatoes. Cover kettle and turn heat to low. Close lid and simmer 40 to 50 minutes, stirring occasionally. Salt lightly, if desired.

8 to 10 servings

Polynesian Beef

4 pounds beef round or
  sirloin steak, trimmed
  and cut in 2-inch cubes
1¼ cups soy sauce
½ cup sweet sherry
½ cup honey
¼ cup vegetable oil

2 tablespoons minced
  fresh ginger
1 teaspoon salt
½ teaspoon cinnamon
¼ teaspoon ground cloves
2 cloves garlic, minced

Place beef cubes in shallow dish. Combine remaining ingredients in small bowl and pour over beef. Cover and refrigerate 2 hours, stirring occasionally. Preheat grill on medium for 10 minutes. Drain beef, reserving marinade. Thread beef onto metal skewers. Place skewers on cooking grid and brush with marinade. Close lid and grill 8 minutes, turning and basting after 4 minutes.

8 to 10 servings

Sukiyaki

3 tablespoons vegetable oil
¾ cup sliced green onions
1 to 1½ pounds boneless
  sirloin beef steak,
  cut in thin strips
1 cup fresh bean sprouts,
  or 1 can (16 ounces)
  bean sprouts, drained
1 can (8 ounces) sliced
  water chestnuts,
  drained
1 package (6 ounces)
  frozen Chinese pea
  pods, thawed

8 cherry tomatoes, cut in
  halves
¼ cup sherry or water
2 tablespoons soy sauce
1 teaspoon cornstarch
1 tablespoon minced fresh
  ginger
½ teaspoon salt
¼ teaspoon freshly ground
  pepper
  Hot cooked rice

Remove cooking grid from grill. Move volcanic rock to one side. Place large cast-iron skillet or heatproof baking dish on grate over one burner. Arrange rocks around skillet. Preheat grill on medium for 10 minutes. Pour oil into skillet. When oil is hot, add green onions and cook until tender, stirring often. Add beef strips; cook and stir until beef is no longer pink. Add bean sprouts, water chestnuts, pea pods, and tomatoes. Close lid and cook 2 to 3 minutes. Combine sherry, soy sauce, cornstarch, ginger, salt, and pepper; stir to dissolve cornstarch. Add to beef mixture. Cook and stir, with lid open, 2 to 3 minutes, or until thickened. Serve over hot rice.

6 servings

Beef Pinwheels

1 beef flank steak
  (about 2 pounds)
  Seasoned instant meat
  tenderizer
1 clove garlic, minced
4 green onions,
  thinly sliced
1 cup dry sherry
⅓ cup soy sauce

¼ cup tomato paste
1 teaspoon Worcestershire
  sauce
½ teaspoon freshly ground
  pepper
8 slices mozzarella cheese
8 fresh or canned peach
  halves, drained

Pound steak between sheets of waxed paper to ½-inch thickness. Sprinkle with meat tenderizer, garlic, and green onions. Roll up, jelly-roll fashion, starting from long side. Cut into 8 pieces and secure each "pinwheel" with wooden skewers. Arrange pinwheels in shallow dish; set aside. Combine sherry, soy sauce, tomato paste, Worcestershire sauce, and pepper. Pour over pinwheels. Cover and refrigerate 2 hours, turning occasionally. Lightly grease cooking grid. Preheat grill on medium for 10 minutes. Drain pinwheels, reserving marinade. Place pinwheels on cooking grid and brush with marinade. Close lid and grill 10 minutes, turning and basting every 3 minutes. Dip cheese slices and peaches in marinade. Arrange cheese over pinwheels; place peaches on cooking grid. Grill peaches 1 minute on each side. After cheese melts, transfer to serving platter and arrange peaches around pinwheels.

8 servings

Indonesian Sate

3 pounds boneless beef or veal, cut in 1½-inch cubes
2 navel oranges, peeled and cut in wedges
2 sweet red peppers, cut in 1-inch chunks
1 cup barbecue sauce
1 cup tomato sauce
½ cup minced celery
1 cup minced onions
2 tablespoons soy sauce
⅓ cup lime juice
1 tablespoon sesame seed, toasted

Alternately thread meat, oranges, and peppers onto metal skewers; set aside. Combine remaining ingredients, except sesame seed, in small bowl. Place skewers in shallow dish and pour sauce over them. Cover and let stand at room temperature 1 hour. Lightly grease right side of cooking grid. Preheat grill on medium for 10 minutes, then turn left side of grill off. Arrange skewers on heated cooking grid and grill 20 minutes, turning and basting with sauce every 5 minutes. Transfer to serving platter and sprinkle with sesame seed before serving.

6 servings

Beef Brisket Barbecue

1 cup red wine or water
1 cup catsup
1 tablespoon instant minced onion
2 tablespoons vinegar
1 tablespoon prepared horseradish
1 tablespoon prepared mustard
1 teaspoon salt
¼ teaspoon freshly ground pepper
1 beef brisket (about 4 pounds)

Combine all ingredients except beef in small bowl. Pour marinade over beef in plastic bag or shallow pan. Seal bag or cover pan. Refrigerate at least 2 hours, turning brisket occasionally. Lightly grease right side of cooking grid. Preheat left side of grill on medium for 10 minutes, then turn to low. Drain beef, reserving marinade. Place beef on right cooking grid. Close lid and grill about 2½ hours, or until desired doneness, basting occasionally with marinade. Transfer to cutting board and cut into thin diagonal slices to serve.

6 to 8 servings

Basic Roast Beef

1 beef sirloin tip, or
   boneless prime rib,
   rib eye, or rump roast,
   rolled and tied
   (3 to 5 pounds)

Beef Marinade (page 108)

Trim fat from roast. Prepare marinade according to directions on page 108. Pour marinade over roast in plastic bag or shallow pan. Seal bag or cover pan. Refrigerate at least 8 hours, turning roast occasionally. Remove cooking grid from grill. Move volcanic rock to one side of grill. Place shallow drip pan in center of grill. Arrange rock around drip pan. Replace cooking grid and grease lightly. Preheat grill on high for 10 minutes. Drain roast, reserving marinade. Insert spit rod through roast. Secure holding forks and check balance. Attach to rotisserie and start motor. Close lid and spit-roast about 5 minutes, or until roast is seared. Turn heat to low and open lid until grill cools to medium. Turn heat to medium-low. Close lid and spit-roast 1¼ to 1½ hours, or until desired doneness, basting occasionally. Transfer to cutting board and cut into thin diagonal slices.

6 to 10 servings

Skewered Liver and Bacon

1 pound calves' liver,
   rinsed and drained
   Cracked peppercorns

1 large onion, cut into
   thin wedges
½ pound bacon (12 slices)

Cut liver into 1½-inch strips, then cut each strip in half. Season with pepper to taste. Place a wedge of onion on each liver piece. Wrap a bacon piece around each liver piece. Thread wrapped liver on 2 or 3 wooden skewers. Grease cooking grid lightly. Preheat grill on medium for 10 minutes, then turn to low. Place skewers on cooking grid or in wire grill basket. Close lid and grill 5 to 7 minutes, turning often, until bacon is crisp and liver is no longer pink.

2 to 3 servings

Savory Chuck Roast

1 beef chuck roast (about 3½ pounds)	¼ teaspoon rosemary
2 cloves garlic, minced	2 tablespoons wine vinegar
2 tablespoons olive or vegetable oil	2 tablespoons lemon juice
1 teaspoon soy sauce	2 tablespoons corn syrup
¼ teaspoon dry mustard	¼ teaspoon Worcestershire sauce

Place roast in large dish; set aside. Sauté garlic in oil in small saucepan until tender. Stir in soy sauce, mustard, and rosemary. Remove from heat. Stir in vinegar, lemon juice, corn syrup, and Worcestershire sauce. Pour sauce over roast. Cover and refrigerate at least 8 hours, turning occasionally. Lightly grease cooking grid. Preheat grill on medium for 10 minutes, then turn left side of grill off and right side to low. Drain roast, reserving marinade. Place roast on right cooking grid. Cover and grill about 25 to 30 minutes, or until desired doneness, turning and basting frequently with reserved marinade.

6 to 8 servings

Ground Beef Special

1 pound lean ground beef	½ teaspoon salt
⅓ cup chopped onion	¼ teaspoon freshly ground pepper
1 can (10¾ ounces) chicken gumbo soup, undiluted	¼ teaspoon chili powder
3 tablespoons catsup	6 hamburger buns, split and buttered
2 teaspoons prepared mustard	

Remove cooking grid from grill. Move volcanic rock to one side of grill. Place large skillet on grate. Arrange rock around skillet. Preheat grill on medium for 10 minutes. Cook beef and onion in skillet, with lid open, about 10 minutes, stirring to break up meat, until beef is no longer pink and onion is tender. Stir in remaining ingredients, except buns. Turn heat to low. Close lid and heat about 10 minutes, stirring occasionally. Serve on hamburger buns.

6 servings

Sesame Chuck Roast

1 boneless chuck roast (about 3 pounds)	½ cup strong coffee
Butter or margarine, softened	½ cup soy sauce
Instant meat tenderizer	1 tablespoon Worcestershire sauce
1 large onion, chopped	1 tablespoon vinegar
	1 tablespoon sesame seed

Rub roast with butter. Pierce well with a fork and sprinkle with meat tenderizer. Combine remaining ingredients and pour over roast in plastic bag or shallow pan. Seal bag or cover pan. Refrigerate at least 1½ hours, turning occasionally. Remove cooking grid from grill. Place shallow drip pan on volcanic rock on right side of grill. Replace cooking grid and lightly grease right cooking grid over drip pan. Preheat grill on high for 10 minutes, then turn left side of grill off and right side to medium-high. Drain roast, reserving marinade. Place roast on heated cooking grid. Close lid and grill 25 to 30 minutes, or until desired doneness, basting occasionally with reserved marinade. Transfer to cutting board and cut into thin diagonal slices to serve.

6 to 8 servings

Garlic Minute Steaks

¼ cup butter or margarine, melted	1 large clove garlic, minced
2 tablespoons Worcestershire sauce	6 beef minute steaks (½ pound each)
2 tablespoons lemon juice	6 slices French bread, toasted
2 teaspoons chopped parsley	Freshly ground pepper
¾ teaspoon celery salt	

Preheat grill on high for 10 minutes. Combine butter, Worcestershire, lemon juice, parsley, celery salt, and garlic. Brush butter sauce on both sides of steaks; reserve any extra sauce. Place steaks in wire grill basket and place on grill. Close lid and grill 2 to 4 minutes, turning once. Sprinkle with pepper to taste. Serve each minute steak on a bread slice; spoon remaining butter sauce over top.

6 servings

Made-to-Order Hamburgers

1½ pounds lean ground beef
¼ teaspoon salt

⅛ teaspoon freshly ground
pepper

Choice of any of the following:

¼ cup chopped parsley
⅓ cup pickle relish
1 teaspoon oregano
⅓ cup chopped dill pickle
½ cup (2 ounces) shredded
Cheddar or American
cheese or crumbled
blue cheese
1 teaspoon chili powder
¼ cup chili sauce or catsup
1 tablespoon steak sauce
1 tablespoon
Worcestershire sauce

¼ cup toasted sesame seed
¼ cup dairy sour cream or
plain yogurt
2 tablespoons minced
onion or chopped
green chilies
Beef Seasoning Salt
(page 111)
6 hamburger buns,
split and buttered

Combine beef, salt, pepper, and choice of optional ingredients; blend well. Shape into 6 patties; set aside. Lightly grease right side of cooking grid. Preheat grill on medium for 10 minutes, then turn left side of grill off. Place hamburgers on right cooking grid. Close lid; grill 5 minutes. Turn burgers and place split sides of buns on grill to toast. Grill 5 to 7 minutes, or until centers of burgers are slightly firm. Sprinkle with Beef Seasoning Salt and serve on toasted buns.

6 servings

Cheeseburger Deluxe

1½ pounds lean ground beef
½ cup tomato juice
½ cup sliced stuffed
green olives
3 tablespoons chopped
parsley
3 tablespoons chopped
onion

½ teaspoon salt
⅛ teaspoon freshly ground
pepper
6 slices American cheese
6 hamburger buns,
split and buttered

Combine all ingredients except cheese and buns; blend well. Shape into 6 patties and set aside. Lightly grease right side of cooking grid. Preheat grill on medium for 10 minutes, then turn left side of grill off. Place hamburgers on right cooking grid. Close lid; grill 5 minutes. Turn burgers and place buns, split side down on grill to toast. Grill 5 to 7 minutes, or until centers of burgers are slightly firm. Place a cheese slice on each burger and grill until cheese is melted. Serve on toasted buns.

6 servings

Lumberjack Burger

1½ pounds lean ground beef
¾ cup rolled oats
¾ cup catsup
1 egg
1 teaspoon salt
¼ teaspoon freshly ground pepper
1 round loaf bread (about 10 inches in diameter), cut horizontally in half and buttered

4 to 6 thin slices Cheddar cheese

Tomato slices
Sliced pickles or pickle relish
Lettuce leaves

Combine beef, oats, catsup, egg, salt, and pepper; blend well. Pat beef mixture into 10-inch circle on double thickness of heavy-duty aluminum foil. Preheat grill on medium for 10 minutes. Lift meat and foil onto cooking grid. Close lid; grill 15 minutes. Place bread, cut side down, on grill to toast. Arrange cheese slices on top of meat and grill 5 minutes, or until cheese is melted. Remove meat and bread from grill. Place meat on bottom half of bread. Top with tomato slices, pickles, lettuce, and top half of loaf. Cut into wedges with a serrated knife and serve.

6 to 8 servings

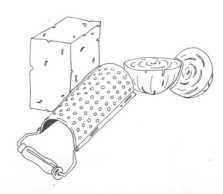

Best of the Barnyard

A perennial favorite, all types of kissin' cousin poultry from chicken to duck to turkey are featured here. We've included the basics, but added the special Structo grill touch. Try tumbled, turned, and spitted poultry; you'll really give friends, family, and the chef, of course, something to crow about.

Tumbled Chicken and Ribs

2 pounds country-style
  pork spareribs
10 chicken thighs
  (2½ pounds)

Salt
Freshly ground pepper

Trim fat from ribs and chicken. Rinse and pat dry with paper towels. Separate ribs into individual pieces. Center round rotisserie basket on spit rod. Layer chicken and ribs in basket, filling no more than two-thirds full; set aside. Remove cooking grid from grill. Place shallow drip pan on volcanic rock in center of grill. Replace cooking grid. Preheat grill on medium for 10 minutes. Attach spit rod to rotisserie, centering basket over drip pan; start motor. Close lid and spit-cook 60 to 90 minutes, or until chicken is tender and ribs are no longer pink near bone. Transfer chicken and ribs to serving platter. Sprinkle with salt and pepper to taste and serve.

8 to 10 servings

Easy Barbecued Chicken

1 broiler-fryer chicken (2½
  to 3 pounds), cut up

1 cup homemade or bottled
  barbecue sauce

Trim fat from chicken, rinse, and pat dry with paper towels. Lightly grease right side of cooking grid. Preheat grill on medium for 10 minutes, then turn off left side of grill. Arrange chicken on right cooking grid. Close lid and grill 35 to 40 minutes, or until chicken is tender, turning twice. Baste with barbecue sauce during last 15 minutes cooking time. If flare-ups occur, move chicken to left cooking grid.

4 servings

TIMING GUIDE FOR COOKING POULTRY

Cut	Size/Weight	Grill Setting	Approx. Total Cooking Time
Chicken			
Whole, Unstuffed	2-3 pounds	Medium-Low .	1-1¼ hours
Whole, Stuffed	2-3 pounds	Low	1¼-1½ hours
Pieces, Halves, and Quarters	2-4 pounds	Medium-Low	40-50 minutes
Cornish Hen	1½ pounds	Low	35-50 minutes
Duckling			
Whole, Unstuffed	3-5 pounds	Medium-Low	1½-2 hours
Whole, Stuffed	3-5 pounds	Medium-Low	2-2½ hours
Turkey			
Whole, Unstuffed	10-14 pounds	Low	20 minutes per pound
Whole, Stuffed	10-14 pounds	Low	25 minutes per pound
Pieces, Halves, and Quarters	4-6 pounds	Low	50-55 minutes

Spitted Stuffed Chicken

1 roasting chicken or capon (4 to 5 pounds)
2 onions, minced
2 cloves garlic, minced
¼ cup butter
½ pound ground pork sausage
1 teaspoon thyme
⅓ cup chopped parsley
1½ cups coarse bread crumbs
1 teaspoon salt
Freshly ground pepper
2 eggs, lightly beaten

Remove neck and giblets from chicken; discard or save for use in soups or gravies. Rinse chicken and pat dry with paper towels. Sauté onions and garlic in butter in large skillet until onion is tender. Add sausage and thyme; cook and stir 5 minutes. Add parsley, bread crumbs, salt, pepper, and eggs; blend well. Add a little more butter if needed for moisture. Lightly stuff cavity and secure with skewers. Tie legs and wings to bird with heavy string. Close neck opening with skewer. Remove cooking grid from grill. Place shallow drip pan on volcanic rock in center of grill. Preheat grill on medium for 10 minutes, then turn to low. Insert spit rod through bird. Secure holding forks and check balance. Attach to rotisserie and start motor. Close lid and spit-roast about 20 minutes per pound, or until chicken is tender. (If roasting chicken unstuffed, allow about 15 minutes per pound.)

4 servings

Lemon Tarragon Chicken

1 broiler-fryer chicken,
cut up (3 to 3½ pounds)
½ cup softened butter or
margarine
2 tablespoons fresh
lemon juice

1 to 2 tablespoons
tarragon
1 teaspoon Dijon-style
mustard

Trim fat from chicken, rinse, and pat dry with paper towels. Combine butter, lemon juice, tarragon, and mustard; blend well. Rub mixture over chicken, reserving any extra for basting. Lightly grease cooking grid. Preheat grill on medium for 10 minutes, then turn left side of grill off and the right side to medium-low. Arrange chicken on heated cooking grid. Close lid and grill 50 minutes, or until chicken is tender, turning and basting often with herb-butter mixture.

4 servings

Orange Glazed Duckling

1 fresh or thawed
frozen duckling
(4½ to 5 pounds)
½ cup frozen orange juice
concentrate, thawed,
undiluted

2 tablespoons soy sauce
2 tablespoons Cointreau
1 teaspoon honey
¼ teaspoon basil
⅛ teaspoon freshly ground
pepper

Remove neck and giblets from duckling; discard or save for use in soups or gravies. Rinse duckling and pat dry with paper towels. Tie legs and wings to bird with heavy string. Close neck opening with skewer. Pierce skin well with fork; set aside. Combine remaining ingredients in saucepan. Bring to a boil. Reduce heat and simmer, stirring constantly, until hot and smooth. Remove cooking grid from grill. Place shallow drip pan on lava rock in center of grill. Replace cooking grid and grease lightly. Preheat grill on medium for 10 minutes, then turn to medium-low. Place duckling, breast side up, on cooking grid over drip pan. Close lid and grill 1½ to 2 hours, or until juices run clear when pierced with fork, basting occasionally with orange glaze. Transfer to serving platter and let stand 10 minutes before serving.

2 to 3 servings

Spitted Whole Turkey

1 turkey (8 to 10 pounds), fresh or thawed if frozen	1 large onion, sliced
	1 bunch parsley
	1 clove garlic, halved
Salt	Butter or margarine
Freshly ground pepper	Paprika

Remove neck and giblets from turkey; discard or save for use in soups or gravies. Rinse turkey and pat dry with paper towels. Sprinkle inside and out with salt and pepper. Fill cavity with onion, parsley, and garlic. Rub skin with small amount of butter, then sprinkle with paprika. Tie legs and wings to bird with heavy string. Close neck opening with skewer. Remove cooking grid from grill. Place shallow drip pan on volcanic rock in center of grill and fill with 1 inch water. Preheat grill on medium for 10 minutes. Insert spit rod through bird. Attach holding forks and check balance. Attach to rotisserie and start motor. Close lid and spit-cook about 2 to 2½ hours, or until center of thigh muscle registers 180°F on meat thermometer. Cover legs and wings with foil if browning too rapidly. Use bulb baster to refill drip pan with water as needed. Let stand 10 minutes before carving. Discard onion, parsley, and garlic before serving.

10 to 12 servings

Turkey Pieces with Sweet Potatoes

6 turkey legs, wings, or thighs	½ cup red currant jelly
	¼ cup port wine
6 medium sweet potatoes, unpeeled, washed and patted dry	¼ cup catsup
	2 tablespoons butter or margarine
Butter or margarine, softened	½ teaspoon Worcestershire sauce

Rinse turkey pieces and pat dry with paper towels; set aside. Rub sweet potatoes with butter and wrap each in heavy-duty aluminum foil; set aside. Combine jelly, wine, catsup, butter, and Worcestershire in small saucepan. Bring to a boil, stirring constantly. Reduce heat and simmer until smooth and hot; set aside. Preheat grill on medium for 10 minutes, then turn left side of grill off. Arrange turkey and sweet potatoes on right cooking grid. Close lid and grill 60 to 75 minutes, or until turkey is tender, turning every 15 minutes. Baste with sauce during last 20 minutes cooking time.

6 servings

Phoenix Spiced Chicken Wings

3 pounds chicken wings, tips removed
1 tablespoon salt
2 teaspoons paprika
1 teaspoon lemon-pepper

1 teaspoon onion powder
½ teaspoon red pepper flakes
½ teaspoon garlic powder
½ teaspoon sage

Rinse chicken wings and pat dry with paper towels. Combine remaining ingredients in paper bag. Add wings, a few at a time, and shake to coat with seasonings. Let wings stand for 1 hour. Lightly grease right side of cooking grid. Preheat grill on medium for 10 minutes, then turn left side of grill off and right side to low. Shake excess seasoning from wings. Place wings on heated cooking grid. Close lid and grill 8 minutes on each side. Serve hot.

4 servings

Herbed Chicken

2 broiler-fryer chickens, quartered (3 to 3½ pounds each)
1 large onion, minced
1 cup dry sherry
½ cup vegetable oil
1 tablespoon Worcestershire sauce

1 teaspoon soy sauce
1 teaspoon lemon juice
1 clove garlic, minced
1 teaspoon thyme
1 teaspoon rosemary
1 teaspoon dillweed

Trim fat from chicken, rinse, and pat dry with paper towels. Arrange chicken in shallow pan. Combine remaining ingredients in small bowl and pour over chicken. Turn chicken to coat all sides. Cover and refrigerate at least 4 hours, turning chicken occasionally. Lightly grease cooking grid. Preheat grill on medium for 10 minutes, then turn to medium-low. Drain chicken, reserving marinade. Arrange chicken on cooking grid. Close lid and grill 40 to 50 minutes, or until chicken is tender, basting frequently with marinade.

8 servings

Grilled Game Hens

4 cornish game hens
½ cup butter or margarine,
  softened
2 tablespoons chopped
  chives
½ teaspoon rosemary

2 tablespoons lemon juice
¼ cup apricot jam, melted
  and strained
8 to 10 fresh or canned
  apricot halves

Split hens in half. Combine butter, chives, and rosemary. Spread butter mixture over skin of hens. Heat lemon juice and leftover butter mixture in small saucepan, until melted. Remove cooking grid from grill. place shallow drip pan on lava rock in center of grill. Replace cooking grid and grease lightly. Preheat grill on low for 10 minutes. Place hen halves, skin side up, on cooking grid over drip pan. Close lid and grill 45 to 50 minutes, or until thighs are tender, basting occasionally with butter sauce. Brush hens with melted jam during last 10 minutes cooking time. Transfer hens to serving platter and garnish with apricot halves.

8 servings

Brandied Chicken

2 broiler-fryer chickens,
  halved (3 to 3½ pounds
  each)
Salt
Freshly ground pepper
½ cup butter or margarine,
  melted
¼ cup lemon juice

6 tablespoons brandy,
  divided
¼ cup packed brown sugar
1 cup pitted sweet dark
  cherries, drained
6 peaches, halved and
  pitted, or 12 canned
  peach halves, drained

Trim fat from chicken, rinse, and pat dry with paper towels. Sprinkle chicken halves with salt and pepper to taste; set aside. Combine butter, lemon juice, 4 tablespoons brandy, and brown sugar in medium bowl. Dip chicken in butter mixture; drain. Combine cherries and peaches in metal pan; set aside. Grease cooking grid lightly. Preheat grill on medium for 10 minutes, then turn to medium-low. Arrange chicken, skin side up, on cooking grid. Close lid and grill 40 to 50 minutes, or until chicken is tender, basting occasionally. During last 10 minutes cooking time, brush fruit with basting sauce and heat on grill 6 to 10 minutes. Transfer chicken to serving platter and garnish with fruit. Carefully pour remaining 2 tablespoons brandy over chicken and fruit. Ignite and spoon flaming fruit over chicken.

4 servings

Oriental Chicken with Potatoes

6 chicken legs and thighs (3 pounds)	1 clove garlic, minced
½ cup vegetable oil	¼ cup butter or margarine
⅓ cup soy sauce	2 large onions, thinly sliced
⅓ cup honey	4 large potatoes, unpeeled, cooked and thinly sliced
3 tablespoons dry sherry	
½ cup thinly sliced green onions	
2 teaspoons minced fresh ginger, or ¾ teaspoon ground ginger	

Trim fat from chicken, rinse, and pat dry with paper towels. Arrange chicken in shallow pan. Combine oil, soy sauce, honey, sherry, green onions, ginger, and garlic in small bowl. Pour over chicken; turn to coat all sides. Cover and refrigerate at least 4 hours, turning chicken occasionally. Lightly grease cooking grid. Preheat grill on medium for 10 minutes, then turn left side off and right side to medium-low. Drain chicken, reserving marinade. Arrange chicken on right cooking grid. Close lid and grill 40 to 50 minutes, or until chicken is tender, basting often with marinade. During last 15 minutes cooking time, melt butter in skillet on other side of cooking grid. Sauté onions in butter about 5 minutes, stirring occasionally, until tender. Add potato slices and cook 10 minutes, or until heated through. Just before serving, stir 2 tablespoons reserved marinade into potatoes. Transfer chicken to serving platter and arrange potato mixture around chicken.

6 servings

From Coney Island to County Fair

Ahhh! The down-home taste of pork! A hot dog with all the trimmings — sauerkraut, mustard, relish, chili, and onions — starts off this chapter. Next, there's an array of pork recipes that just might win awards at the next County Fair. Try Barbecued Pork Roast (page 58), Apricot Stuffed Pork Chops (page 57), or Glazed Ham Steak (page 62). We've topped it off, with several versions of everybody's favorite: ribs, of course.

County Fair Hot Dogs

4 jumbo hot dogs (2 ounces each)	Mustard, pickle relish, chopped onions,
4 hot dog rolls, split	sauerkraut, chili

Preheat grill on medium for 10 minutes. Place jumbo hot dogs on cooking grid. Add buns, cut side down. Close lid and grill 8 to 10 minutes, turning frequently. Remove buns as soon as toasted. Serve hot dogs in toasted buns with your choice of toppings.

4 servings

Apricot Stuffed Pork Chops

6 thick pork center loin chops	¼ cup catsup
Freshly ground pepper	2 tablespoons chopped onion
1 can (17 ounces) apricot halves, drained; ½ cup syrup reserved	2 tablespoons vegetable oil
	1 tablespoon lemon juice
	½ teaspoon dry mustard

Have butcher cut pockets in chops. Sprinkle chops with pepper to taste. Insert 2 apricot halves in each pocket. Cut remaining apricots into small pieces; set aside. Preheat grill on medium for 10 minutes. Place chops on cooking grid and grill about 25 minutes, or until no longer pink near bone, turning once. (Or, place in wire grill basket and grill.) Meanwhile combine reserved apricot syrup, apricot pieces, and remaining ingredients in heavy saucepan. Simmer sauce on grill 15 minutes. Brush chops with sauce 5 minutes before chops are done. Pass remaining sauce with chops.

6 servings

TIMING GUIDE FOR COOKING PORK
Lid Closed

Cut	Size/Weight	Grill Setting	Approx. Total Cooking Time
Fresh			
Chops: Rib or Loin	½ inch thick	Low	15-20 minutes
	1 inch thick	Low	25-30 minutes
Kabobs	1-1½ inch thick	Low	15-20 minutes
Roast, Bone In	5-8 pounds	Low	2½-3½ hours (170°F)
Roast, Boneless	5-8 pounds	Low	2-3 hours (170°F)
Cured			
Ham Steaks	½ inch thick	Medium	12-15 minutes
	1 inch thick	Medium	13-18 minutes
Ham Roast, Cook-Before-Eating, Boneless	5-8 pounds	Low	2-2½ hours (160°F)
Ham Roast, Fully Cooked, Bone-in	6-12 pounds	Low	1½-2 hours (140°F)
Hot Dogs		Medium	7 minutes
Spareribs	4 pounds	Low	1-1¼ hours
Country-Style Ribs	4 pounds	Low	45-60 minutes
Bacon	4 slices	High on griddle	5-8 minutes
Canadian-Style	6-8 slices	High on griddle	
	¼ inch thick	High on griddle	3 minutes
	½ inch thick	High on griddle	5 minutes

Barbecued Pork Roast

1 boneless smoked pork shoulder (2 to 3 pounds)

½ cup barbecue sauce (optional)

Remove cooking grid from grill. Place shallow drip pan on volcanic rock in center of grill. Replace cooking grid. Preheat grill on medium for 10 minutes. Remove casing from pork shoulder. Insert spit rod through pork. Secure holding forks and check balance. Attach to rotisserie and start motor. Close lid and spit-cook about 30 minutes, or until interior registers 170°F on meat thermometer. Baste with barbecue sauce, if desired, during last 15 minutes cooking time. Slice and serve.

6 to 9 servings

Barbecued Pork Chops

6 thick pork center loin chops	1 teaspoon ground ginger
3 tablespoons soy sauce	¼ teaspoon freshly ground pepper
⅓ cup orange marmalade	1 clove garlic, minced

Trim fat from chops. Combine remaining ingredients and brush over chops, reserving any extra for basting. Remove cooking grid from grill. Place shallow drip pan on volcanic rock in center of grill. Replace cooking grid and grease lightly. Preheat grill on high for 10 minutes, then turn to low. Place chops on cooking grid over drip pan. Close lid and grill 25 to 30 minutes, or until chops are no longer pink, turning and basting often.

6 servings

Spicy Pork Kabobs

3 pounds boneless pork, cut in 1-inch cubes	1 teaspoon ground ginger
1 can (16 ounces) pineapple chunks, drained, liquid reserved	1 clove garlic, minced
	2 tart apples, cored and cut in thick wedges
⅓ cup soy sauce	12 small whole onions, parboiled for 5 minutes

Arrange pork cubes in shallow dish. Combine pineapple liquid, soy sauce, ginger, and garlic and pour over pork. Cover and refrigerate at least 2 hours, stirring occasionally. Add apples and onions to pork and stir to coat. Alternately thread pork, pineapple chunks, onions, and apples on skewers. Brush with marinade; set aside. Lightly grease right side of cooking grid. Preheat right side of grill on medium for 10 minutes, then turn to low. Place kabobs on cooking grid. Close lid and grill 20 minutes, or until pork is no longer pink, turning and basting often with marinade.

6 servings

Cranberry Glazed Pork Roast

1 boneless pork roast
(3 pounds), rolled and
tied
1 teaspoon pepper

1 can (8 ounces) jellied
cranberry sauce
1 teaspoon dry mustard

Remove cooking grid from grill. Place shallow drip pan on volcanic rock in center of grill. Preheat grill on medium for 10 minutes, then turn to low. Sprinkle pork roast with pepper. Insert spit rod through roast. Secure with holding forks and check balance. Attach to rotisserie and start motor. Close lid and spit-cook about 1 hour 15 minutes, or until interior of meat registers 170°F on meat thermometer. Melt cranberry sauce in small saucepan; stir in mustard. Baste roast with cranberry sauce during last 20 minutes cooking time.

8 to 10 servings

Oriental Spareribs

4 to 6 pounds lean
country-style pork
spareribs

Oriental Barbecue Sauce
(page 109)

Trim fat from ribs. Remove cooking grid from grill. Place shallow drip pan on volcanic rock in center of grill. Replace cooking grid. Preheat grill on medium for 10 minutes, then turn to low. Place ribs on cooking grid over drip pan. Grill, with lid open, about 45 minutes, or until fat cooks off, turning often. Brush ribs with sauce. Close lid and grill 20 minutes, or until ribs are no longer pink near bone, turning and basting after 10 minutes. Baste with sauce before serving.

4 to 6 servings

Spareribs on a Spit

4 to 5 pounds lean
country-style pork
spareribs

Barbecue sauce

Trim fat from ribs. Thread ribs onto spit rod, accordion-style. Secure with holding forks and check balance. Remove cooking grid from grill. Place shallow drip pan on volcanic rock in center of grill. Replace cooking grid. Preheat grill on medium for 10 minutes, then turn to low. Attach spit rod to rotisserie and start motor. Close lid and grill 30 to 35 minutes, or until ribs are no longer pink near bone. Baste often with barbecue sauce during last 15 minutes cooking time.

4 to 6 servings

Sweet and Sour Spareribs

6 pounds lean
country-style pork
spareribs
1½ cups red wine vinegar
1 can (6 ounces) frozen
pineapple juice
concentrate, thawed,
undiluted

½ cup packed dark brown
sugar
3 tablespoons vegetable oil
3 tablespoons minced
green pepper
1½ teaspoons soy sauce
1 clove garlic, minced

Trim fat from ribs; set aside. Combine remaining ingredients in saucepan. Simmer 10 minutes, stirring until thick and smooth; set aside. Remove cooking grid from grill. Place shallow drip pan on volcanic rock in center of grill. Replace cooking grid. Preheat grill on medium for 10 minutes, then turn to low. Place ribs on cooking grid over drip pan. Grill, with lid open, about 45 minutes, or until fat cooks off, turning often. Brush ribs with sauce. Close lid and grill 20 minutes, or until ribs are no longer pink near bone, turning and basting after 10 minutes. Transfer to serving platter, brush with sauce, and serve.

6 servings

San Antonio Ribs

4 pounds lean
    country-style pork
    spareribs
Freshly ground pepper
2 cups tomato juice
Juice of 2 limes
3 tablespoons
    Worcestershire sauce

1 tablespoon chili powder
2 teaspoons red pepper
    flakes
1 teaspoon salt
1 clove garlic, pressed
½ teaspoon ground cumin

Trim fat from ribs. Sprinkle with pepper to taste. Place ribs in shallow pan. Combine remaining ingredients and pour over ribs. Cover and refrigerate at least 8 hours, turning ribs occasionally. Drain ribs, reserving marinade. Remove cooking grid from grill. Place shallow drip pan on volcanic rock in center of grill. Replace cooking grid. Preheat grill on medium for 10 minutes, then turn to low. Place ribs on cooking grid over drip pan. Close lid and grill 45 to 60 minutes, or until ribs are no longer pink near bone, turning often and basting with marinade during last 20 minutes cooking time.

4 servings

Glazed Ham Steak

⅓ cup packed brown sugar
1 teaspoon dry mustard
½ teaspoon allspice

1 fully cooked ham steak
    (about 2 pounds)
Whole cloves

Combine brown sugar, mustard, and allspice. Score top of ham at 1-inch intervals to create diamond pattern. Insert a clove in center of each diamond. Preheat grill on medium for 10 minutes, then turn to low. Sprinkle one side of ham with half the brown sugar mixture. Place ham, sugar side up, on cooking grid. Close lid and grill 10 minutes; turn. Sprinkle with remaining brown sugar mixture and grill 10 minutes. Discard cloves before serving.

4 to 6 servings

Hawaiian Ham Kabobs

¼ cup orange juice
¼ cup butter or margarine, melted
1 tablespoon corn syrup
2 teaspoons minced fresh ginger
1 tablespoon grated orange peel

1 pound baked ham, cut in 1-inch cubes
1 fresh pineapple, cut in chunks, or 16 chunks canned pineapple, drained
1 orange, unpeeled, cut into 6 wedges

Combine orange juice, butter, corn syrup, ginger, and orange peel in bowl large enough to hold ham. Add ham and stir lightly to coat. Cover and refrigerate 2 hours, stirring occasionally. Drain ham, reserving marinade. Alternately thread ham, pineapple, and orange wedges on skewers; set aside. Preheat grill on medium for 10 minutes. Place kabobs on cooking grid. Close lid and grill 15 minutes, turning and basting often with marinade.

4 servings

Spicy Kielbasabobs

¼ cup horseradish mustard
¼ cup chili sauce
2 tablespoons taco seasoning mix
2 tablespoons water
2 tablespoons vegetable oil
6 precooked smoked kielbasa, cut in thirds

1 can (16 ounces) whole potatoes, drained
2 green peppers, cut in chunks
3 ears fresh corn, husked and cut in 2-inch chunks

Combine mustard, chili sauce, taco seasoning, water, and oil; set aside. Thread kielbasa, potatoes, green peppers, and corn onto 4 metal skewers. Lightly grease cooking grid. Preheat grill on medium for 10 minutes, then turn to low. Place kabobs on cooking grid. Close lid and grill about 15 minutes, or until sausage is hot and vegetables are tender, turning skewers often and basting sausage during last 5 minutes cooking time with mustard sauce.

4 servings

Franks in Barbecue Sauce

¾ cup butter or margarine
1 cup chopped onions
2 tablespoons all-purpose
   flour
⅓ cup packed brown sugar
1 teaspoon dry mustard
1 teaspoon paprika
½ teaspoon chili powder
½ teaspoon salt

1 cup catsup
1 cup beer or water
⅓ cup vinegar
3 tablespoons
   Worcestershire sauce
1 tablespoon lemon juice
12 skinless frankfurters
12 frankfurter buns, split

Remove cooking grid from grill. Move volcanic rock to one side of grill. Place large saucepan on grate. Melt butter in saucepan over low heat. Add onions; sauté until tender. Combine flour, brown sugar, mustard, and spices. Stir into onions. Stir in catsup, beer, vinegar, Worcestershire, and lemon juice. Bring to a boil, stirring constantly. Add frankfurters to sauce. Cover saucepan. Close lid and grill about 5 minutes, or until heated through. Remove saucepan from grate and replace cooking grid. Place saucepan on cooking grid. Brush buns with some of the sauce. Place buns, cut sides down, on cooking grid to toast. Serve frankfurters in buns, topped with sauce.

12 servings

Recipe can be doubled.

Brats in Beer

6 to 8 fresh bratwurst
1 can (12 ounces) beer
½ to 1 cup chopped onions

6 to 8 bratwurst buns,
   split
Prepared mustard

Preheat grill on medium for 10 minutes. Combine bratwurst, beer, and ½ cup onion in large saucepan. Place on cooking grid and bring to a boil. Turn heat to low and simmer about 10 minutes. Remove bratwurst from pan and place on the cooking grid. Move pan to back of grill. Close lid and grill 6 to 8 minutes, turning occasionally to brown all sides. Serve immediately, or return bratwurst to pan until ready to serve. Serve on bratwurst buns, topped with mustard; sprinkle with additional onion, if desired.

6 to 8 servings

Bacon Cheese Dogs

1 package (16 ounces) frankfurters	10 hot dog buns, split
5 slices American cheese	½ cup catsup
10 strips bacon	2 tablespoons pickle relish, drained

Cut deep lengthwise slit in frankfurters. Stack cheese slices and cut into 6 strips. Stuff hot dogs with cheese strips. Wrap bacon strip around each hot dog and secure with wooden picks; set aside. Preheat grill on medium for 10 minutes, then turn to low. Place hot dogs on cooking grid. Add buns, cut side down. Close lid and grill 8 to 10 minutes, turning hot dogs often. Watch buns carefully and remove as soon as they are toasted. Blend catsup and relish in small bowl. Serve hot dogs in toasted buns, topped with catsup mixture.

10 servings

Skewered Bratwurst

6 precooked bratwurst, cut in thirds	½ teaspoon paprika
¼ cup half and half	¼ teaspoon lemon-pepper
2 tablespoons prepared mustard	1 can (16 ounces) sauerkraut, undrained
½ teaspoon instant minced onion	

Thread bratwurst pieces onto 4 metal skewers. Combine half and half, mustard, onion, paprika, and lemon-pepper; set aside. Empty sauerkraut into saucepan. Remove cooking grid from grill. Place shallow drip pan on volcanic rock in center of grill. Replace cooking grid and grease lightly. Preheat grill on medium for 10 minutes, then turn to low. Place sauerkraut and skewers on cooking grid. Brush skewers with mustard sauce. Close lid and grill 7 to 8 minutes, or until hot, turning frequently. Drain sauerkraut and serve topped with a skewer of bratwurst.

4 servings

Lamb
For All Seasons

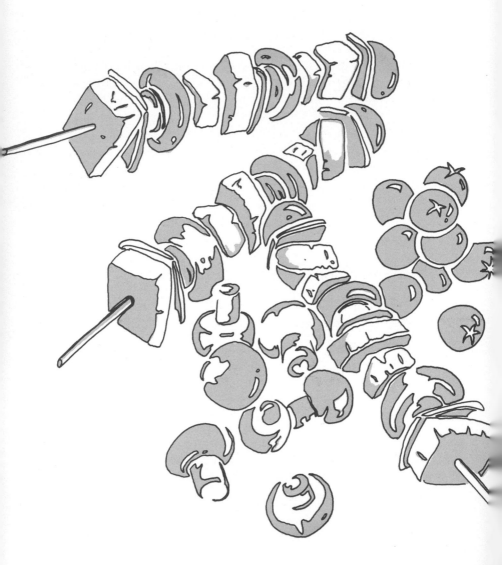

Festive lamb is the focal point of this chapter. Kabobs are fun and so easy to do, yet all your guests will think you fussed for hours. From the elegance of a Crown Roast of Lamb (page 70) to the simplicity of Lamb Patties (page 68), you'll be winning praises from family and friends. What's more, the kitchen stays *cool* and so do you!

Herbed Lamb Chops

8 thick loin lamb chops	½ teaspoon garlic powder
2 tablespoons lemon juice	Salt
¾ teaspoon basil	Freshly ground pepper

Trim fat from chops. Slash edges every 1½ inches to prevent chops from curling. Brush chops with lemon juice and sprinkle with basil and garlic powder. Lightly grease cooking grid. Preheat grill on medium for 10 minutes, then turn to low. Place chops on cooking grid. Close lid and grill 5 minutes. Turn and grill 5 minutes, or until desired doneness. Add salt and pepper to taste before serving.

4 servings

Classic Shish Kabob

2 pounds boneless lamb shoulder, cut in 1½-inch cubes	½ teaspoon oregano
	1 green pepper, cut in 1½-inch cubes
1 large onion, cut in wedges	12 large mushroom caps
½ teaspoon salt	12 cherry tomatoes
¼ teaspoon freshly ground pepper	

Place lamb in shallow dish. Top with onion. Combine salt, pepper, and oregano; sprinkle over lamb and onion. Cover and refrigerate at least 4 hours. Lightly grease cooking grid. Preheat grill on medium for 10 minutes, then turn to low. Thread lamb cubes onto 6 metal skewers. Thread onion, green pepper, and mushrooms onto 2 skewers and tomatoes onto 1 skewer. Place kabobs on cooking grid. Close lid and grill 10 to 15 minutes, turning twice, until vegetables are tender-crisp and lamb is well browned.

6 servings

TIMING GUIDE FOR COOKING LAMB
Lid Closed

Cut	Size/ Weight	Doneness	Grill Setting	Approx. Total Cooking Time
Chops;	1 inch	Rare	Medium	8-10 minutes
Shoulder,	thick	Medium	Medium	10-15 minutes
Rib, or		Well Done	Medium	15-18 minutes
Loin	1½ inch	Rare	Medium	10-12 minutes
	thick	Medium	Medium	12-18 minutes
		Well Done	Medium	18-20 minutes
Steaks	1 inch	Rare	Medium	12-15 minutes
	thick	Medium	Medium	18 minutes
		Well Done	Medium	25 minutes
	1½ inch	Rare	Medium	16 minutes
	thick	Medium	Medium	20 minutes
		Well Done	Medium	30 minutes
Kabobs	1½ inch	Rare	Low	12 minutes
	thick	Medium	Medium	20 minutes
		Well Done	Medium	18 minutes
Leg, Bone-In	5-8 pounds	Rare (140°F)	Low	75-90 minutes
		Medium (160°F)	Low	1½-1¾ hours
		Well Done (170°F)	Low	1¾-2 hours
Leg, Boneless	4-6 pounds	Rare (140°F)	Low	50-60 minutes
		Medium (160°F)	Low	60-70 minutes
(Rotisserie)		Well Done (170°F)	Low	70-90 minutes
Crown Roast	5-8 pounds	Rare (140°F)	Low	60-90 minutes
		Medium (160°F)	Low	1¾-2 hours
		Well Done (170°F)	Low	2-2½ hours

Lamb Patties

1 pound ground lamb, or
  ¾ pound lamb plus ¼
  pound lean ground beef
1 teaspoon curry powder
½ teaspoon ground
  coriander

½ teaspoon onion powder
½ teaspoon lemon pepper
4 slices bacon

Combine all ingredients, except bacon, in bowl; blend well. Shape mixture into four 4-inch patties. Wrap bacon slice around outside edge of each patty and fasten with toothpick. Preheat right side of grill on medium for 10 minutes. Place patties on right cooking grid. Close lid and grill about 5 minutes. Turn and grill 6 to 8 minutes, or until patties are well browned and bacon is done. Remove tooth-picks and serve.

4 servings

Lemon Lamb Shoulder Chops

4 lamb shoulder chops
  (¾ to 1 inch thick)
⅔ cup vegetable oil
⅓ cup lemon juice
1 small onion, chopped

½ teaspoon salt
½ teaspoon paprika
½ teaspoon lemon pepper
  Lemon slices
  Parsley sprigs

Place lamb chops in shallow dish. Combine oil, lemon juice, onion, salt, paprika, and lemon-pepper. Pour over chops and turn to coat. Cover and refrigerate at least 4 hours, turning occasionally. Remove cooking grid from grill. Place shallow drip pan on volcanic rock in center of grill. Replace cooking grid and grease lightly. Preheat grill on medium for 10 minutes. Drain chops, reserving marinade. Place chops on cooking grid over drip pan. Close lid and grill 8 to 10 minutes, or until well browned with pink centers, turning and basting once. Garnish with lemon slices and parsley.

4 servings

Stuffed Leg of Lamb

1 boneless leg of lamb
  (4 to 6 pounds)
¾ cup chopped parsley
3 large cloves garlic,
  minced

1 tablespoon oregano
  Grated peel of 1 lemon
½ teaspoon salt
  Dash crushed red pepper
  Juice of 1 lemon

Gently open leg of lamb. Combine parsley, garlic, oregano, lemon peel, salt, and red pepper. Sprinkle into leg opening. Roll up and tie with heavy string. Preheat grill on high for 10 minutes, then turn to medium-low. Insert spit rod through lamb. Secure holding forks and check balance. Attach to rotisserie and start motor. Close lid and spit-cook 1½ to 2 hours, or until thickest part of meat registers 160°F on meat thermometer, basting occasionally with lemon juice. Let stand 10 minutes before slicing.

8 to 10 servings

Minted Leg of Lamb

1 boneless leg of lamb
(4 to 6 pounds)
1 cup olive oil
1 cup dry white wine
1 teaspoon dry mustard
1 teaspoon oregano

2 tablespoons soy sauce
½ teaspoon freshly ground
pepper
1 teaspoon rosemary
2 cloves garlic, minced
2 tablespoons chopped mint

Pound lamb to an even thickness. Combine remaining ingredients and pour over lamb in plastic bag or shallow pan. Seal bag or cover pan. Cover and refrigerate at least 8 hours, turning occasionally. Remove cooking grid from grill. Place shallow drip pan on volcanic rock in center of grill. Replace cooking grid and grease lightly. Preheat grill on high for 10 minutes, then turn to medium-low. Drain lamb, reserving marinade. Place lamb on cooking grid over drip pan. Close lid and grill 30 to 40 minutes, turning and basting often with marinade. Let stand 10 minutes before slicing.

8 to 10 servings

Crown Roast of Lamb

1 lamb crown roast
(4 to 5 pounds)
2 cloves garlic, split
⅓ cup lemon juice
2 teaspoons oregano
½ teaspoon salt
¼ teaspoon lemon-pepper

½ cup chopped celery
½ cup chopped onion
½ cup chopped apple
3 cups dry bread crumbs
½ cup raisins
¼ cup butter, melted
¾ cup chicken broth

Rub surface of roast with garlic. Tie roast securely with heavy string. Combine lemon juice, oregano, salt, and lemon-pepper. Brush lemon mixture over roast; set aside. Combine remaining ingredients in casserole dish; blend well. Cover casserole. Remove cooking grid from left side of grill. Place shallow drip pan on volcanic rock. Replace cooking grid and grease lightly. Preheat grill on medium for 10 minutes, then turn to low. Place roast, bone up, on greased cooking grid. Place stuffing opposite roast. Close lid and grill about 45 minutes, inserting meat thermometer during last 10 minutes, until thickest part of meat registers 140°F to 145°F. Stir stuffing once during cooking time. Transfer lamb to serving platter and fill center with stuffing.

6 servings

Leg of Lamb in Wine Marinade

1 boneless leg of lamb (4 to 6 pounds), rolled and tied	2 cups dry red wine 1 cup French dressing

Place lamb in large roasting pan. Combine wine and French dressing; pour over lamb, turning to coat. Cover and refrigerate 8 hours, turning occasionally. Remove cooking grid from grill. Move volcanic rock to one side. Place shallow drip pan on grate. Arrange rock around pan. Preheat grill on high for 10 minutes, then turn to medium-low. Drain lamb, reserving marinade. Insert spit rod through lamb. Secure holding forks and check balance. Attach to rotisserie and start motor. Close lid and spit-cook 1½ to 2 hours, or until thickest part of meat registers 160°F on meat thermometer, basting often with marinade during last 15 minutes. Let stand 10 minutes before slicing.

8 to 10 servings

Grilled Lamb Shanks

4 to 6 pounds lamb shanks, cracked	2 tablespoons chopped parsley
¾ cup white wine	2 teaspoons chopped mint
¼ cup honey	2 cloves garlic, pressed
2 tablespoons lemon juice	½ teaspoon lemon pepper

Place lamb shanks in 6-quart saucepan and add water to cover. Bring to a boil; reduce heat and simmer 30 minutes. Drain and set aside to cool. Place lamb shanks in deep bowl. Combine remaining ingredients and pour over lamb, turning to coat. Cover and refrigerate 8 hours, turning occasionally. Remove cooking grid from grill. Place shallow drip pan on volcanic rock in center of grill. Replace cooking grid and grease lightly. Preheat grill on medium for 10 minutes. Drain lamb shanks, reserving marinade. Place lamb on cooking grid over drip pan. Close lid and grill 15 to 20 minutes, or until tender, turning and basting twice.

4 to 6 servings

Catch of the Day

If you've never looked to seafood as fair game for outdoor cooking, now's the time to reexamine the possibilities. Cooked on the grill, fish takes on a new flavor and texture that will convert those who "never touch it." Shellfish and other treasures of the deep are excellent, too. And why not celebrate your discoveries with a full-blown Backyard Clambake (page 74).

Barbecued Swordfish Steak

½ cup soy sauce
½ cup orange juice
¼ cup catsup
2 tablespoons lemon juice
¼ cup chopped parsley
1 teaspoon freshly ground
  pepper

1 teaspoon oregano
2 cloves garlic, minced
½ teaspoon dry mustard
6 swordfish steaks
  (8 ounces each)

Combine all ingredients, except swordfish steaks, in small bowl. Place steaks in plastic bag or shallow glass dish. Pour sauce over steaks. Seal bag or cover dish. Let stand at least 2 hours, turning occasionally. Preheat grill on medium for 10 minutes, then turn to low. Drain fish, reserving sauce. Place steaks in lightly greased wire grill basket. Place basket on cooking grid. Close lid and grill 20 minutes, turning after 10 minutes; baste often with sauce.

6 servings

For equally delicious results, try substituting halibut, salmon, or ocean perch for the swordfish steaks.

Boiled Whole Lobster

4 quarts water
6 slices lemon
6 whole peppercorns
2 tablespoons salt

½ cup butter
1 tablespoon lemon juice
2 live lobsters
  (1 pound each)

Combine water, lemon slices, peppercorns, and salt in 6-quart kettle. Remove cooking grid from grill. Move volcanic rock to one side. Place kettle on grate and cover. Arrange rock around kettle. Bring to a boil on high with lid open. Melt butter in small saucepan, then pour off milk solids to clarify. Stir in lemon juice; set aside. Plunge lobsters, head first, into boiling water; cover. Close lid and heat until water returns to boil. Turn heat to low. Simmer 5 to 10 minutes, or until lobster is done. Reheat butter sauce during last 3 minutes on warming rack. Remove lobsters from water; drain, split, and clean. Serve with butter sauce.

2 servings

Backyard Clambake

24 littleneck or steamer
   clams in shell,
   scrubbed and rinsed
9 quarts cold water,
   divided
9 tablespoons salt,
   divided
4 pieces chicken
   Salt
   Freshly ground pepper

4 ears corn, unhusked
4 small lobster tails
1 bunch seaweed or
   parsley
4 whole small Bermuda
   onions (quartered,
   if large)
   Fresh parsley
1 cup melted butter

Soak clams in 3 quarts water and 3 tablespoons salt for 15 minutes. Drain and repeat soaking twice, using remaining water and salt. Preheat grill on high for 10 minutes, then turn to medium-low. Place chicken on cooking grid, skin side down. Close lid and grill 10 minutes, turning once. Remove chicken from grill. Season chicken with salt and pepper to taste; set aside. Peel husks back from corn but do not detach. Remove silk; pull husks back over corn. Tear off 4 large sheets of heavy-duty aluminum foil; fold each sheet in half. Divide seaweed or parsley among foil. Cut four 18-inch squares of cheesecloth. Place 1 ear corn, 6 clams, 1 piece chicken, 1 onion, and 1 lobster tail on each piece of cheesecloth. Bring ends of cheesecloth up and tie together. Place each bundle on seaweed and fold foil over to seal. Place packets on cooking grid. Close lid and grill 45 minutes, or until chicken is tender, clams open, and lobster is done. Arrange fresh parsley on serving plates. Remove food from packets and place on parsley. Serve with individual cups of melted butter, salt, and pepper.

4 servings

For a delicious and economical substitute, use four fish fillets for lobster.

Barbecued Shrimp

6 tablespoons butter or margarine, melted
2 tablespoons lemon juice
2 tablespoons chopped parsley
½ teaspoon curry powder
1 clove garlic, minced
½ teaspoon salt
Dash freshly ground pepper
2 pounds large shrimp, shelled and deveined

Tear off six 12-inch sheets of heavy-duty aluminum foil; grease lightly. Combine all ingredients, except shrimp, in bowl large enough to hold shrimp. Add shrimp and stir to coat. Divide shrimp among foil. Fold edges of foil up and over to seal. Preheat grill on medium for 10 minutes. Place foil packets on cooking grid. Close lid and grill 6 to 8 minutes, turning packets once. Serve directly from packets if desired.

6 servings

Summer Scallops

2 tablespoons butter or margarine
1 clove garlic, minced
¼ cup minced shallots or green onions
1 pound sea scallops
Dry vermouth
Hot cooked rice

Remove cooking grid. Move volcanic rock to one side of grate. Place large saucepan on grate. Add butter and melt over high heat. Add garlic and shallots and sauté until lightly browned. Add scallops and stir to coat. Add dry vermouth just to cover scallops. Cover and simmer over medium-low heat 5 to 8 minutes. Serve with rice.

4 servings

Grill-Baked Flounder Fillets

2 pounds flounder fillets	¼ teaspoon salt
1 lemon, cut in half	⅛ teaspoon freshly ground
2 tablespoons parsley	pepper
flakes	⅛ teaspoon oregano
2 tablespoons instant	½ cup slivered almonds
minced onion	3 tablespoons butter or
2 tablespoons minced celery	margarine

Rub fillets with one lemon half; set aside. Combine parsley, onion, celery, salt, pepper, and oregano; set aside. Tear off a sheet of heavy-duty aluminum foil large enough to hold fish. Fold sides up to form shallow pan; grease lightly. Place fillets in pan. Squeeze remaining lemon half over fillets; and rub parsley mixture into fish. Sprinkle with almonds and dot with butter. Cover with foil. Preheat grill on medium for 10 minutes, then turn left side of grill off and right side to low. Place pan on left cooking grid. Close lid and grill 10 to 15 minutes, or until fish flakes when tested with fork.

4 servings

Sesame Fish

1 whole fish, such as	½ cup butter, melted, or
striped bass, sea bass,	vegetable oil
salmon, trout, pike,	½ cup sesame seed
or red snapper	Salt
(2 to 3 pounds), cleaned	Freshly ground pepper
2 tablespoons lemon juice	

Sprinkle cavity of fish with lemon juice. Brush skin with butter and dip in sesame seed to coat all sides. Reserve any extra butter and sesame seed. Lightly grease cooking grid. Preheat grill on medium for 10 minutes, then turn to low. Place fish on cooking grid. (Or place in wire grill basket sprayed with nonstick cooking spray.) Close lid and grill 8 minutes, or until fish flakes when tested with fork, brushing with butter and dipping in sesame seed after 4 minutes. Season with salt and pepper to taste.

4 servings

Grill-Baked Red Snapper

½ cup butter or margarine,
melted
2 pounds red snapper
fillets
1 lemon, cut in half

½ teaspoon garlic powder
½ teaspoon onion powder
¼ teaspoon salt
¼ teaspoon paprika
½ cup coarsely chopped
fresh dill

Tear off a sheet of heavy-duty aluminum foil twice as large as needed to hold fish. Brush a little of the melted butter over foil. Place fish in center of foil and brush with remaining butter. Squeeze lemon over fish. Sprinkle with garlic powder, onion powder, salt, paprika, and dill. Fold edges of foil up and over to seal; set aside. Preheat grill on medium for 10 minutes, then turn to low. Place foil packet on cooking grid. Close lid and grill 8 to 10 minutes, turning after 5 minutes, until fish flakes when tested with fork.

4 servings

If available, you may substitute sea, striped, or black bass for red snapper.

Sablefish Teriyaki

2 to 3 pounds sablefish
fillets
½ cup dry sherry or
apple juice
¼ cup soy sauce

2 tablespoons lemon juice
1 tablespoon vegetable oil
2 tablespoons minced onion
½ teaspoon minced fresh
ginger

Tear off 2 sheets of heavy-duty aluminum foil large enough to hold fillets. Fold sides up to form shallow pans; grease lightly. Place fillets, skin sides down in pans; set aside. Combine remaining ingredients in small saucepan. Simmer 2 to 3 minutes, or until slightly thickened. Brush sauce over fish. Let stand at room temperature for 30 minutes. Preheat grill on medium for 10 minutes, then turn to low. Place fish in pans on cooking grid. Close lid and grill 8 minutes basting often with sauce, until fish flakes when tested with fork.

4 to 6 servings

Marinated Salmon Steaks

1 cup dry white wine
¼ cup soy sauce
1 heaping teaspoon
   Dijon-style mustard

1 large clove garlic,
   minced
4 salmon steaks
   (8 ounces each)

Combine wine, soy sauce, mustard, and garlic in small bowl. Place steaks in single layer in shallow glass dish. Pour marinade over steaks. Let stand for at least 30 minutes, turning once. Preheat grill on medium for 10 minutes, then turn to low. Tear off sheet of heavy-duty aluminum foil large enough to hold steaks in single layer. Fold sides up to form shallow pan and grease lightly. Drain salmon, reserving marinade. Arrange steaks in pan and place on cooking grid. (Or place steaks in wire grill basket sprayed with nonstick cooking spray.) Close lid and grill about 12 minutes, or until fish flakes when tested with fork, turning after 6 minutes and basting with marinade. Baste again before serving.

4 servings

Savory Salmon Steaks

4 salmon steaks
   (8 ounces each)
½ teaspoon salt
1 teaspoon lemon-pepper

¼ cup Italian salad
   dressing
1 teaspoon minced onion
   Chopped parsley

Tear off sheet of heavy-duty aluminum foil large enough to hold all steaks. Fold sides up to form shallow pan; grease lightly. Sprinkle steaks with salt and lemon-pepper. Place in foil pan and set aside. Combine salad dressing and onion; set aside. Preheat grill on medium for 10 minutes, turn to low. Brush steaks on both sides with dressing mixture. Place steaks in pan and place on cooking grid. Close lid and grill 12 minutes, or until steaks flake when tested with fork, turning after 6 minutes and basting often with dressing mixture. Remove to serving platter. Sprinkle with parsley and serve.

4 servings

Foil-Wrapped Mackerel Steaks

½ cup chopped onion
½ cup chopped green
   pepper
2 tablespoons butter or
   margarine
½ cup catsup

¼ teaspoon garlic powder
¼ teaspoon salt
1 bay leaf
4 mackerel steaks
   (8 ounces each)

Sauté onion and green pepper in butter in skillet until tender-crisp. Add catsup, garlic powder, salt, and bay leaf; simmer 10 minutes, stirring occasionally. Discard bay leaf. Tear off 4 sheets of heavy-duty aluminum foil, each large enough to hold 1 steak; grease lightly. Place 1 fish steak in center of each sheet of foil. Pour sauce over steaks. Fold edges of foil up and over to seal; set aside. Preheat grill on medium for 10 minutes, then turn to low. Place packets on cooking grid. Close lid and grill 15 minutes, or until fish flakes when tested with fork.

4 servings

Butterflied Trout with Almonds

4 whole trout, cleaned and
   scaled (8 to 10 ounces
   each)
1 bottle (8 ounces)
   Italian salad dressing

¼ cup butter or margarine
½ cup slivered almonds

Bone trout without cutting completely through back of fish. Cut off and discard fins. Carefully spread fish open. Place in single layer in large shallow glass pan. Pour dressing over fish. Cover and let stand about 30 minutes. Lightly grease cooking grid. Preheat grill on medium for 10 minutes, then turn to low. Drain fish, reserving dressing. Place fish, skin side down, on cooking grid and brush with dressing. Close lid and grill 10 minutes, or until fish flakes when tested with a fork, turning once and basting occasionally with dressing. Melt butter in heavy saucepan on grill. Stir in nuts and sauté until lightly browned. Serve butter sauce over fish.

4 servings

The Old Smokehouse

The pace of life seems to ease up a bit when we recall the marvelous aroma of food slow-smoking at home. The gas grill lets you bring back those days with ease. Hickory Smoked Salmon (page 85), Smoked Turkey Breast (page 82), and Smoked Spareribs (page 84) are just a few of the many possibilities offered in this chapter. Smoke cooking takes time, but is it ever worth it!

Smoked Whole Capon

1 capon or roasting chicken (5 to 7 pounds)
Salt
1 stalk celery with leaves, cut in chunks
1 small onion, sliced
¼ cup loosely packed parsley sprigs

Soak wood chips in water to cover for at least 30 minutes. Remove neck and giblets from capon; discard or save for use in soups and gravies. Rinse and pat dry with paper towels. Sprinkle with salt. Place celery, onion, and parsley in cavity. Tie legs and wings to bird with heavy string. Close neck opening with skewer. Remove cooking grid from grill. Move volcanic rock to one side. Place deep foil drip pan on grate and fill with about 2 inches water. Preheat grill on high for 10 minutes. Form wood chip log (see page 9) and place opposite drip pan on volcanic rock. Close lid and heat 10 to 20 minutes, or until chips begin to smolder. Turn off burner under drip pan; turn other side to low. Refill drip pan with water, if needed. Replace cooking grid and grease lightly. Place capon on cooking grid over drip pan. Close lid and smoke about 2½ hours, or until bird is tender. (Smoked poultry is slightly pinker near bone than conventional roasted poultry.) Add more wood chips as needed. Discard vegetables and parsley before serving.

6 to 8 servings

Smoked Turkey Breast

1 turkey breast (5½ to
6 pounds), bone in

1 cup bottled teriyaki
sauce

Rinse turkey breast, trim fat, and place in plastic bag or shallow
dish. Pour teriyaki sauce over turkey. Seal bag or cover dish.
Refrigerate at least 8 hours, turning occasionally. Soak 3 cups
wood chips in water to cover for at least 30 minutes. Remove
cooking grid from grill. Move volcanic rock to one side. Place deep
foil drip pan on grate and fill with about 1 inch water. Preheat grill
on high for 10 minutes. Form wood chip log (see page 9) and place
opposite drip pan on volcanic rock. Close lid and heat on high 10 to
20 minutes, or until chips begin to smolder. Turn off burner under
drip pan; turn other side to low. Refill drip pan with water, if
needed. Replace cooking grid and grease lightly. Drain turkey,
reserving marinade. Place turkey on cooking grid over drip pan.
Close lid and smoke 2 to 3 hours, or until turkey is tender, basting
every 30 minutes. Add more wood chips as needed. Baste and
smoke 10 more minutes. For a stronger smoked flavor, refrigerate
turkey overnight after cooking.

10 to 12 servings

Smoked Barbecued Pork Roast

1 lean boneless pork roast
(3 to 4 pounds),
rolled and tied

Tomato-Wine Marinade
(page 107)

Place roast in plastic bag or shallow dish. Pour marinade over
roast. Seal bag or cover dish. Refrigerate at least 3 hours, turning
occasionally. Soak 3 cups hickory wood chips in water to cover for
at least 30 minutes. Remove cooking grid from grill. Move volcanic
rock to one side. Place shallow drip pan on grate and fill with 1 inch
water. Preheat grill on high for 10 minutes. Form wood chip log
(see page 9) and place opposite drip pan on volcanic rock. Close lid
and heat 10 to 20 minutes, or until chips begin to smolder. Turn off
burner under drip pan; turn other side to low. Refill drip pan with
water, if needed. Replace grid and grease lightly. Drain roast,
reserving marinade. Place roast on cooking grid over drip pan.
Close lid and smoke about 1½ to 2 hours (30 minutes per pound) or

until center of meat registers 170°F on meat thermometer, basting occasionally with marinade. Add more wood chips as needed. For best results, cover and refrigerate for 1 day before serving.

6 to 9 servings

Smoked Duck

1 duckling (5 to 6 pounds)	1 onion, quartered
1½ cups Orange Sauce	Cornstarch
(page 110)	
1 apple, cored and	
quartered	

Remove neck and giblets from duck; discard or save for use in soups and gravies. Rinse duck and pat dry with paper towels. Place duck in plastic bag or shallow dish. Pour Orange Sauce into and over duck to coat lightly, reserving extra sauce. Seal bag or cover dish. Refrigerate at least 8 hours. Soak wood chips in water to cover for 30 minutes. Remove cooking grid from grill. Move volcanic rock to one side. Place deep foil drip pan on grate and fill with about 1 inch water. Preheat grill on high for 10 minutes. Form wood chip log (see page 9) and place opposite drip pan on volcanic rock. Close lid and heat 10 to 20 minutes, or until chips begin to smolder. Turn both sides of grill to low. Refill drip pan with water, if needed. Replace cooking grid. Drain duck, discarding marinating sauce. Prick skin well with fork. Place apple and onion in cavity. Tie legs and wings to bird with heavy string. Close neck opening with skewer. Place duck on cooking grid over drip pan. Close lid and smoke about 2½ hours (30 minutes per pound), or until leg joint moves freely. Add more wood chips as needed. Before serving dissolve cornstarch in reserved orange sauce in small saucepan (Use 1 scant teaspoon per ½ cup of sauce). Cook over low heat, stirring constantly, until thickened. Discard apple and onion; serve duck with Orange Sauce.

3 to 4 servings

Smoked Spareribs

¼ cup vinegar
¼ cup Worcestershire sauce
¼ cup butter or margarine, melted
2 tablespoons salt
¼ teaspoon hot pepper sauce
¼ teaspoon garlic powder
4 to 5 pounds pork spareribs

Soak 3 cups wood chips in water to cover for at least 30 minutes. Combine vinegar, Worcestershire, butter, salt, hot pepper sauce, and garlic powder. Brush sauce over ribs, reserving any extra. Remove cooking grid from grill. Move volcanic rock to one side. Place deep foil drip pan on grate and fill with about 2 inches water. Preheat grill on high for 10 minutes. Form wood chip log (see page 9) and place opposite drip pan on volcanic rock. Close lid and heat on high 10 to 20 minutes, or until chips begin to smolder. Turn both sides of grill to low. Refill drip pan with water, if needed. Replace cooking grid. Place spareribs on cooking grid over drip pan. Close lid and smoke about 1½ hours (15 to 30 minutes per pound), or until ribs are no longer pink near bone. Add more wood chips as needed. Brush with vinegar sauce and smoke 5 minutes. Turn, brush with sauce, and smoke 5 minutes. Transfer to cutting board and cut into two-rib pieces.

5 to 6 servings

Loin backribs are a good choice for smoking or rotisserie cooking, since they have a thick layer of meat. The meatiest cut is called country-style. Allow about ¾ pound per serving.

Hickory Smoked Salmon

2 tablespoons butter or
   margarine, melted
2 tablespoons lemon juice
2 tablespoons chopped dill,
   or 1 teaspoon dried
   dillweed

1 dressed whole salmon
   (5 to 7 pounds)
Lemon pepper

Soak 3 cups hickory chips in water to cover for at least 30 minutes. Combine butter, lemon juice, and dill. Brush butter mixture over fish. Sprinkle with lemon-pepper. Remove cooking grid from grill. Move volcanic rock to one side. Place shallow drip pan on grate and fill with 1 inch water. Preheat grill on high for 10 minutes. Form wood chip log (see page 9) and place opposite drip pan on volcanic rock. Close lid and heat 10 to 20 minutes, or until chips begin to smolder. Turn both sides of grill to low. Refill drip pan with water, if needed. Replace cooking grid. Place salmon on cooking grid over drip pan. Close lid and smoke until fish flakes when tested with a fork, basting with butter mixture occasionally. Add more wood chips as needed. For best results, smoke fish about 3 hours. Wrap tightly and refrigerate or freeze.

6 to 10 servings

Farmstand Favorites

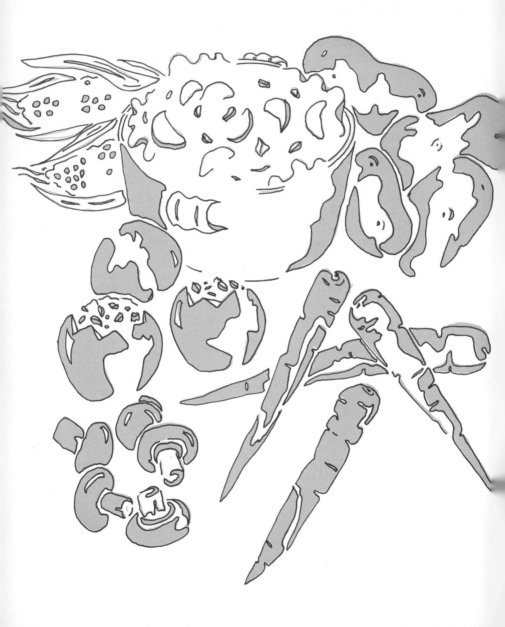

Treat that colorful display of farm-fresh vegetables with great respect and take home some summer harvest for your next backyard meal. Corn on the Cob (page 87), Bacon Wrapped Baked Potatoes (page 97), and Squash and Tomato Bake (page 93) make great grill-alongs with your favorite main dish. And try one of our delicious rice dishes for more on-the-side grillings to round out your summer roundup.

Foil-Baked Tomatoes

6 medium-size firm
　　tomatoes
Salt

Freshly ground pepper
1 onion, thinly sliced

Remove stem ends from tomatoes and cut in half crosswise. Sprinkle with salt and pepper to taste. Place onion slices between tomato halves and secure with wooden picks. Wrap tomatoes individually in heavy-duty aluminum foil. Preheat right side of grill on medium for 10 minutes. Place tomatoes on cooking grid. Close lid and grill 10 to 15 minutes, or until hot. Or, alternately, grill with other food, placing tomatoes around edge of cooking grid.

6 servings

Corn on the Cob

6 ears corn, unhusked
¼ cup butter or margarine,
　　melted

Butter
Salt
Freshly ground pepper

Peel husks back from corn without removing them. Remove silk and pull husks back over ears. Tie husks around corn with string. Soak in cold water 10 to 15 minutes. Drain corn, discarding water. Place each ear on a sheet of heavy-duty aluminum foil. Brush with melted butter. Wrap corn in foil. Preheat grill on medium for 10 minutes. Place corn on cooking grid. Close lid and grill 20 to 25 minutes, turning every 5 minutes. Serve with additional butter, salt, and pepper.

6 servings

TIMING GUIDE FOR COOKING VEGETABLES
Lid Closed

Food	Amount/ Weight	Preparation	Grill Setting	Approx. Total Cooking Time
Asparagus	1 pound	Whole, in foil packet	Medium	15-20 min.
Carrots	1 pound	Thickly sliced, in foil packet	Medium	25-30 min.
	1 pound	Young whole, in foil	Medium	50-55 min.
Corn on the	4-6 ears	Husked, foil-wrapped	Medium	20-25 min.
Cob		Unhusked	Medium	20-25 min.
Eggplant	1-2 pounds	Stuffed halves, foil-wrapped	Low	20-25 min.
Green Beans	1 pound	Whole, in foil packet	Medium	20-25 min.
Mushrooms	½ pound	Whole or sliced in foil packet	Low	10-12 min.
	8-16	Large whole, stuffed	Medium	8-10 min.
Onions	½ pound	Sliced, in foil packet	Medium	20-25 min.
	3-4	Large whole, foil-wrapped	Medium	25-30 min.
Potatoes	½ pound each	Baked, with or without foil wrap	Medium	50-60 min.
Summer	¾-1 pound	Whole, foil-wrapped	Medium	25-40 min.
Squash		Stuffed halves, foil-wrapped	Medium	25-35 min.
Zucchini	1 pound	Sliced, in foil packet	Low	10-12 min.
Tomatoes	2-3 medium	Whole, foil-wrapped	Medium	10-15 min.
Winter Squash	1½ pounds	Halved, foil-wrapped	Medium	25-35 min.
Mixed	2 cups	Sliced, in foil packet	Medium	20-25 min.
Vegetables		Diced, in foil packet	Medium	20-25 min.

Mushrooms in Foil

½ pound fresh mushrooms
2 tablespoons butter or
  margarine
2 tablespoons chopped
  parsley

1 teaspoon instant
  minced onion

Clean mushrooms; cut in halves or slices if desired. Tear off a sheet of heavy-duty aluminum foil. Place mushrooms in center of foil. Dot with butter and sprinkle with parsley and onion. Fold edges of foil up and over to seal. Preheat grill on high for 5 minutes, then turn left side of grill off and right side to low. Place packet on left cooking grid. Close lid and grill 12 minutes, turning packet every 5 minutes. Serve over grilled steak.

4 servings

Armenian Rice Pilaf

1 cup broken-up vermicelli
1 cup long-grain rice
1 cup chopped celery
1 cup chopped onions
¼ cup butter or margarine
2 cloves garlic, minced
2¼ cups water

2 teaspoons instant
   chicken bouillon
   granules
1 teaspoon salt
⅛ teaspoon freshly ground
   pepper

Combine vermicelli, rice, celery, onions, butter, and garlic in 3-quart casserole. Remove cooking grid from grill. Move volcanic rock to one side. Place casserole on grate. Arrange rock around dish. Cook on medium, with lid open, 10 to 12 minutes, stirring occasionally, until pasta and rice are light brown and vegetables tender. Stir in remaining ingredients. Cover casserole and turn heat to low. Close lid and cook about 20 minutes, or until liquid is absorbed. Fluff with fork and serve.

6 servings

Outdoor Pilaf

⅓ cup butter or margarine
1 cup long-grain rice
1 clove garlic, minced
3 cups water
1 tablespoon instant
   beef bouillon granules

¼ teaspoon rosemary
¼ cup raisins
2 tablespoons slivered
   almonds, toasted

Combine butter, rice, and garlic in 2-quart casserole. Remove cooking grid from grill. Move volcanic rock to one side. Place casserole on grate. Arrange rock around dish. Cook and stir on medium, with lid open, until rice is golden. Stir in water, bouillon, and rosemary. Cover casserole and turn heat to low. Close lid and cook 15 to 20 minutes, or until liquid is absorbed. Fluff with fork, sprinkle with raisins and almonds, and serve.

4 servings

Hash Brown Potato Casserole

4 cups frozen southern-style hashed brown potatoes
1 package (8 ounces) cream cheese, softened
1 can (10¾ ounces) cream of celery soup, undiluted

¼ cup chopped onion
1 jar (2 ounces) sliced pimiento, drained
⅓ cup milk
½ cup (2 ounces) grated Cheddar cheese

Combine all ingredients, except Cheddar, in 9 × 13-inch casserole; stir to blend. Cover casserole. Preheat grill on medium for 10 minutes, then turn left side of grill off. Place casserole on left cooking grid. Close lid and bake 50 to 60 minutes, or until potatoes are tender and sauce thickened. Remove from grill and sprinkle cheese on top.

8 to 10 servings

Rice and Mushroom Bake

1⅓ cups instant rice
1¼ cups cold water
½ cup sliced fresh mushrooms
⅓ cup minced onion
1 teaspoon Worcestershire sauce

½ teaspoon salt
¼ teaspoon white pepper
3 tablespoons butter or margarine

Tear off 36-inch sheet of heavy-duty aluminum foil; fold in half. Form a pouch by molding foil around fist. Stir together all ingredients, except butter, in small bowl. Pour into foil pouch. Dot with butter. Fold edges of foil up and over to seal. Preheat grill on high for 10 minutes, then turn left side off and right side to medium-low. Place pouch on right cooking grid. Close lid and grill 10 to 15 minutes, or until liquid is absorbed. Open pouch and fluff with fork before serving.

4 servings

East-West Vegetable Packets

1 package (10 ounces)
  frozen asparagus
1 can (8 ounces) sliced
  water chestnuts,
  drained
3 tablespoons teriyaki
  sauce

1 teaspoon minced fresh
  ginger
¼ teaspoon ground cloves
1 package (6 ounces)
  frozen Chinese
  pea pods

Preheat grill on medium for 10 minutes, then turn to medium-low. Tear off two 24-inch sheets of heavy-duty aluminum foil; stack to form double thickness. Place frozen asparagus in center of foil. Arrange water chestnuts on top. Combine teriyaki sauce, ginger, and cloves and sprinkle over vegetables. Arrange pea pods on top. Enclose an ice cube in packet. Fold edges of foil up and over to seal. Place packet on cooking grid. Close lid and grill 20 minutes, or until vegetables are hot.

6 servings

Skewered Squash and Mushrooms

¼ cup butter or margarine
¼ teaspoon salt
¼ teaspoon lemon-pepper
8 small onions, parboiled
4 small pattypan squash,
  quartered

1 green pepper,
  cut in chunks
8 large mushroom caps

Melt butter in small saucepan. Stir in salt and lemon-pepper; set aside. Alternately thread onions, squash, green pepper, and mushrooms onto 4 metal skewers. Preheat grill on medium for 10 minutes, then turn left side of grill off. Arrange skewers on right cooking grid and brush with butter sauce. Close lid and grill 15 to 20 minutes, or until tender, turning and basting often.

4 servings

Cabbage and Corned Beef

1 small head cabbage (2 pounds)	3 tablespoons beer
½ pound corned beef, thinly sliced	Freshly ground pepper
1 medium onion, thinly sliced	1 bay leaf

Preheat grill on medium for 10 minutes. Tear off two 24-inch sheets of heavy-duty aluminum foil; stack to make double thickness. Cut cabbage from top into 8 wedges without cutting through core. Place cabbage in center of foil. Tuck corned beef and onion in between wedges. Sprinkle with beer and pepper. Top with bay leaf. Fold edges of foil up and over to seal. Place packet on cooking grid. Close lid and grill 35 to 45 minutes, or until cabbage is tender. Discard bay leaf before serving.

4 servings

Hot German Potato Salad

4 slices bacon	¼ teaspoon freshly ground pepper
1 cup chopped celery	
½ cup chopped onion	¼ teaspoon paprika
1 tablespoon flour	¾ cup water
¼ cup vinegar	4 cups sliced, cooked potatoes
2 tablespoons sugar	
1 teaspoon dry mustard	Chopped parsley
½ teaspoon salt	

Place bacon slices in large skillet. Remove cooking grid from grill. Move volcanic rock to one side of grill. Place skillet on grate. Arrange rock around skillet. Cook on medium, turning often, until bacon is crisp. Drain bacon on paper towels. Add celery and onion to drippings. Turn heat to low. Cook and stir until tender but not browned. Add flour and blend well. Stir in vinegar, sugar, mustard, salt, pepper, paprika, and water. Cook and stir until thickened. Gently stir in potatoes. Cover skillet. Close lid and cook about 10 minutes, or until heated through. Crumble bacon over top and sprinkle with parsley.

4 servings

Parmesan Zucchini and Tomatoes

3 zucchini, sliced
2 tomatoes, seeded
  and diced
½ teaspoon oregano
½ teaspoon salt

½ teaspoon garlic powder
3 tablespoons grated
  Parmesan cheese
3 tablespoons butter or
  margarine

Tear off large sheet of heavy-duty aluminum foil. Arrange zucchini and tomatoes in center of foil. Sprinkle with oregano, salt, garlic powder, and cheese. Dot with butter. Fold edges of foil up and over to seal. Preheat grill on medium for 10 minutes, then turn left side off and right side to low. Place packet on heated cooking grid. Close lid and grill 20 to 25 minutes, or until zucchini is tender, turning every 5 minutes.

6 servings

Squash and Tomato Bake

2 medium summer squash,
  cut in ½-inch slices
2 medium tomatoes,
  cut in wedges
1 medium onion,
  thinly sliced
½ teaspoon salt

⅛ teaspoon freshly ground
  pepper
2 tablespoons chopped
  parsley
¼ teaspoon oregano
2 tablespoons olive or
  vegetable oil

Tear off a large sheet of heavy-duty aluminum foil. Arrange half of squash, tomatoes, and onion in center of foil. Sprinkle with half of salt, pepper, parsley, and oregano. Repeat layers with vegetables and seasonings. Drizzle oil over top. Fold edges of foil up and over to seal. Preheat grill on high for 5 minutes, then turn left side of grill off and right side to low. Place packet on left cooking grid. Close hood and grill 10 to 15 minutes, or until vegetables are tender.

4 servings

Savory Carrots and Potatoes

4 small potatoes, peeled
and sliced
1 medium onion,
thinly sliced
4 carrots, thinly sliced
2 tablespoons chopped
parsley

1 teaspoon Italian
seasoning
⅛ teaspoon freshly ground
pepper
¼ teaspoon salt
2 tablespoons butter

Preheat grill on medium for 10 minutes. Tear off two 24-inch sheets of heavy-duty aluminum foil; stack to make double thickness. Arrange potatoes, onion, and carrots on foil. Sprinkle with seasonings. Dot with butter. Enclose 3 ice cubes in packet. Fold edges of foil up and over to seal. Place packet on cooking grid. Close lid and grill 25 to 30 minutes, or until vegetables are tender, turning packet once. Stir before serving.

4 servings

Steamed Cauliflower with Cheese

1 medium head cauliflower
(about 2 pounds),
broken into flowerets
2 teaspoons lemon juice
½ teaspoon salt
¼ teaspoon freshly ground
pepper

2 tablespoons butter or
margarine
½ cup (2 ounces) shredded
sharp Cheddar cheese

Tear off large sheet of heavy-duty aluminum foil. Arrange cauliflower in center of foil. Sprinkle with lemon juice, salt, and pepper. Dot with butter. Enclose 2 ice cubes in packet. Fold edges of foil up and over to seal. Preheat grill on medium for 10 minutes, then turn left side of grill off and right side to medium. Place packet on right cooking grid. Close lid and grill 25 to 30 minutes, or until tender. Open packet and sprinkle cheese over cauliflower, then reseal loosely. Close lid and grill 2 minutes, or until cheese is melted.

4 servings

Spinach Salad

8 slices bacon
¼ cup vinegar
1 tablespoon sugar
½ teaspoon salt
    Dash freshly ground
    pepper
4 green onions,
    thinly sliced

½ cup sliced fresh
    mushrooms
1 pound fresh spinach,
    cleaned and torn in
    bite-size pieces

Remove cooking grid from grill. Place wok or large cast-iron skillet on volcanic rock in center of grill. Cook bacon over medium heat until crisp. Remove bacon from wok with slotted spoon and drain on paper towels. Drain off all but 2 tablespoons drippings. Stir in vinegar, sugar, salt, and pepper. Bring to a boil and remove from grill. Stir until slightly cooled. Add bacon, green onions, mushrooms, and spinach to warm dressing. Toss lightly and serve immediately.

6 servings

Herbed Carrots

8 young carrots, peeled
1 small onion, sliced
1 tablespoon butter or
    margarine

¼ teaspoon basil
½ teaspoon salt
⅛ teaspoon freshly ground
    pepper

Tear off a sheet of heavy-duty aluminum foil. Arrange carrots and onion in center of foil. Dot with butter and sprinkle with basil, salt, and pepper. Enclose an ice cube in packet. Fold edges of foil up and over to seal. Preheat grill on high for 5 minutes, then turn left side of grill off and right side to low. Place packet on left cooking grid. Close lid and grill 50 to 55 minutes, or until carrots are tender, turning every 10 minutes.

3 to 4 servings

For a flavor change, substitute dillweed, parsley, savory, or chives for basil.

Grilled Potato Slices

4 large russet potatoes, unpeeled, scrubbed and rinsed	Butter or margarine, melted Garlic salt

Cut potatoes lengthwise into ¼-inch slices. Brush generously with melted butter and sprinkle with garlic salt. Lightly grease cooking grid. Preheat grill on medium for 10 minutes. Arrange potato slices on cooking grid, or place in wire grill basket. Close lid and grill about 20 minutes, or until browned, turning frequently.

4 to 6 servings

Parslied New Potatoes

1 pound new potatoes, scrubbed and rinsed	2 tablespoons minced parsley
½ teaspoon salt	2 tablespoons butter or margarine
⅛ teaspoon freshly ground pepper	

Cut a 1-inch strip around center of each potato. Tear off a large sheet of heavy-duty aluminum foil. Place potatoes in center of foil. Sprinkle with salt, pepper, and parsley. Dot with butter. Enclose an ice cube in packet. Fold edges of foil up and over to seal. Preheat grill on high for 5 minutes, then turn left side of grill off and right side to low. Place packet on left cooking grid. Close lid and grill 30 to 40 minutes, or until potatoes are tender.

4 servings

Baked Potatoes in Foil

4 medium russet potatoes (5 to 6 ounces each) Butter or margarine Salt Freshly ground pepper	Choice of toppings: Sour cream, bacon bits, chopped chives, sliced green onions, chopped parsley, grated Parmesan cheese

Wash potatoes, pat dry, and pierce well with fork. Wrap individually in heavy-duty aluminum foil. Preheat grill on medium for 10 minutes, then turn to low. Place potatoes on cooking grid. Close lid and bake 30 minutes, or until tender, turning every 5 minutes. To serve, open foil, slash potatoes, and fluff with fork. Season with butter, salt, and pepper to taste. Add your choice of toppings.

4 servings

For a crisper skin, place unwrapped potatoes directly on cooking grid and grill as above.

Bacon-Wrapped Baked Potatoes

4 baking potatoes, scrubbed and rinsed	8 thin slices onion
2 tablespoons butter or margarine	Dash freshly ground pepper
	8 slices bacon

Preheat grill on medium for 10 minutes, then turn to medium low. Tear off 4 sheets of heavy-duty aluminum foil. Cut potatoes in half lengthwise. Spread one side of potatoes with butter. Top with an onion slice and sprinkle with pepper. Top with other potato half. Wrap two slices bacon around each potato. Wrap potatoes in foil. Place potatoes on warming rack at back of grill. Close lid and bake 50 to 60 minutes, or until potatoes are tender. Carefully remove foil and serve.

4 servings

Hearty Baked Beans

2 slices bacon, diced	½ cup maple syrup
½ cup chopped onion	2 tablespoons catsup
2 cans (16 ounces each) pork and beans	1 teaspoon salt
½ cup packed brown sugar	1 teaspoon ginger
	1 teaspoon dry mustard

Remove cooking grid from grill. Move volcanic rock to one side of grill. Place 2-quart casserole on grate in center of grill. Arrange rock around casserole. Preheat grill on medium for 10 minutes. Combine bacon and onion in casserole. Cook and stir until bacon is cooked and onion is tender. Stir in remaining ingredients. Cover casserole and remove from grill. Spread volcanic rock across grate with long-handled tongs. Replace cooking grid. Place casserole on cooking grid. Close lid and bake 30 to 35 minutes, or until hot and bubbly, stirring once. Add more catsup if beans are too dry.

6 servings

Wrapped
and Ready

Are you a fan of the Reuben sandwich? If so, this chapter is for you. All kinds of special sandwiches can be prepared on your gas grill. Most are wrapped in foil before heating. Expecting a crowd? Go ahead and prepare dozens of sandwiches in advance. Heat them on the grill at the last minute. Our variation on the Reuben sandwich, Corned Beef Jumble is found below.

Corned Beef Jumble

½ small onion, chopped	2 eggs, hard-cooked and
½ green pepper, chopped	coarsely chopped
1 tablespoon butter or	¼ cup mayonnaise
margarine	¼ cup chili sauce
12 ounces corned beef,	8 hamburger rolls, split
coarsely chopped	
1 cup (4 ounces) coarsely	
chopped American	
cheese	

Sauté onion and green pepper in butter in skillet until tender-crisp. Combine all ingredients, except rolls, in bowl. Divide corned beef mixture among rolls. Wrap each sandwich in heavy-duty aluminum foil. Preheat grill on medium for 10 minutes, then turn to low. Place sandwiches on cooking grid. Close lid and grill 6 to 10 minutes, or until sandwiches are heated through and cheese is melted.

8 servings

For make-ahead ease, prepare sandwiches, wrap, and freeze. Use straight from the freezer, increasing grill time to 8 to 12 minutes.

Hero Sandwich

1 loaf (1 pound) French bread, split lengthwise in half

½ cup butter or margarine, softened

⅓ cup thousand island salad dressing

1 small onion, thinly sliced

1 green pepper, sliced in thin rings

2 ounces boned cooked chicken breast, thinly sliced

4 ounces summer sausage, thinly sliced

4 ounces boiled ham, thinly sliced

8 ounces Swiss or Cheddar cheese, sliced

1 cup alfalfa sprouts

Preheat grill on medium for 10 minutes. Spread both halves of bread with butter. Place on cooking grid, cut side down. Grill, with lid open, 1 to 2 minutes, or until toasted. Remove from grill. Turn heat to low. Spread bottom half of bread with dressing. Layer remaining ingredients on bread and reassemble loaf. Wrap in double thickness of heavy-duty aluminum foil. Place loaf on cooking grid. Close lid and grill 8 to 12 minutes, or until cheese is melted.

4 servings

Ham and Cheese in Foil

½ cup butter or margarine, softened

3 tablespoons prepared mustard

1 tablespoon poppy seed

1 tablespoon Worcestershire sauce

1 tablespoon grated onion

4 onion or sesame seed rolls, split

4 slices boiled ham

4 slices Swiss cheese

Combine butter, mustard, poppy seed, Worcestershire, and onion; blend well. Spread butter mixture on rolls. Place one slice each of ham and cheese in each roll. Wrap each sandwich in heavy-duty aluminum foil. Preheat grill on medium for 10 minutes, then turn to low. Place sandwiches on cooking grid. Close lid and grill 6 to 10 minutes, or until sandwiches are heated through and cheese is melted.

4 servings

Salami and Tomato Quiche

Pastry for 10-inch
pie crust, unbaked
1 cup shredded provolone
or mozzarella cheese
1½ cups peeled, seeded,
diced, and drained
tomatoes
4 ounces sliced hard
salami, chopped

4 green onions, thinly
sliced, with tops
¾ cup milk
4 large eggs,
lightly beaten
1 teaspoon oregano
½ teaspoon garlic powder
⅛ teaspoon freshly ground
pepper

Line 10-inch pie plate or quiche pan with pastry, making high rim around edge. Seal edge and flute. Prick bottom and sides of crust well. Preheat grill on high 10 minutes, then turn left side of grill off and invert a pan on left cooking grid. Place pie plate on inverted pan. Close lid and bake 5 minutes. Remove pastry shell from grill. Spread cheese, tomatoes, and salami in bottom of shell. Sprinkle with green onions. Mix milk, eggs, oregano, garlic powder, and pepper in small bowl. Carefully pour milk mixture over contents of pastry shell. Return to grill and bake 10 minutes. Turn heat to low. Close lid and bake 30 to 35 minutes, or until knife inserted near center comes out clean. Let stand 10 minutes before serving.

6 to 8 servings

Easy Beer Bread

3 cups self-rising flour
(do not substitute
all-purpose flour)
3 tablespoons sugar

1 can (12 ounces) beer
1 tablespoon butter or
margarine, melted

Grease 9 × 5-inch loaf pan; set aside. Preheat grill on medium for 10 minutes, then turn left side of grill off and invert a baking pan on right cooking grid. Combine flour, sugar, and beer in mixing bowl; blend well. Pour batter into prepared pan. Pour melted butter over top of bread. Place bread on inverted pan. Turn heat to medium-low. Close lid and bake 55 to 60 minutes, rotating pan after 30 minutes, until loaf is golden brown and sounds hollow when lightly tapped. Cool in pan about 5 minutes before turning out of pan. Cut into thick slices and serve.

1 loaf

Backyard Pizza

1 frozen pizza

Preheat grill on high for 10 minutes. Remove wrapper from pizza and place on large baking sheet or heavy-duty aluminum foil. Turn left side of grill off and invert a pan on right cooking grid. Place pizza on inverted pan. Close lid and bake according to package directions, rotating pizza once.

1 pizza

Brown-and-Serve Rolls

1 package (1 dozen)
  brown-and-serve rolls

1 egg
2 tablespoons water

Transfer rolls, if necessary, to metal pan. Preheat grill on medium for 10 minutes, then turn left side of grill off and invert a pan on right cooking grid. Lightly beat egg and water. Brush egg mixture on top of rolls. Place roll pan on top of inverted pan. Turn heat to medium. Close lid and grill 10 minutes, or until golden brown, rotating pan after 5 minutes. Turn out of pan and serve.

12 rolls

Garlic Bread

½ cup butter or margarine,
  softened
2 tablespoons grated
  Parmesan cheese

2 cloves garlic, pressed
1 loaf (1 pound)
  French bread

Combine butter, cheese, and garlic; blend well. Cut loaf diagonally into 1-inch slices without cutting through bottom of loaf. Spread butter mixture on slices. Spread any remaining butter mixture over top of loaf. Wrap loaf in double thickness of heavy-duty aluminum foil. Preheat grill on high for 10 minutes, then turn left side of grill off and right side to medium-low. Place loaf on right cooking grid. Close lid and grill 15 minutes, turning once. Or, alternately, heat with other grilled food, placing loaf on warming rack at back of grill.

1 loaf

Spicy English Muffins

½ cup butter or margarine,
    softened
1 teaspoon chili powder

½ teaspoon onion salt
4 English muffins, split

Combine butter and seasonings; blend well. Spread muffins with butter mixture. Preheat grill on high for 10 minutes, then turn left side off and right side to medium. Place muffins in wire grill basket on right cooking grid. Grill about 3 minutes on each side, or until golden brown. Or, alternately, toast directly on grill, turning with tongs.

4 servings

Bubble Bread

2 loaves (1 pound each)
    frozen white bread
    dough
1 cup sugar

4 teaspoons cinnamon
1 teaspoon nutmeg
1 cup butter or margarine,
    melted

Thaw dough and let rise according to package directions. Grease 10-inch tube pan; set aside. Combine sugar, cinnamon, and nutmeg. Roll dough into 1½-inch balls. Dip balls into melted butter, then roll in sugar-cinnamon mixture. Layer balls in prepared pan. Cover and let rise in warm, draft-free place about 50 minutes, or until doubled in bulk. Preheat grill on medium for 10 minutes, then turn left side of grill off and invert a pan on right cooking grid. Place bread pan on top of inverted pan. Turn heat to medium-low. Close lid and bake about 45 minutes, or until loaf is golden brown and sounds hollow when lightly tapped. Cool in pan 10 minutes before turning out onto serving plate.

1 ring loaf

Hot Herb Bread

1 cup butter or margarine, softened
¾ cup minced chives
¾ cup chopped parsley
1 teaspoon Italian seasoning
¼ teaspoon salt
1 clove garlic, finely minced
2 loaves (1 pound each) French bread, split lengthwise in half

Combine butter, chives, parsley, Italian seasoning, salt, and garlic; blend well. Spread butter mixture over cut sides of bread; reassemble loaves. Wrap each loaf in double thickness of heavy-duty aluminum foil. Preheat grill on high for 10 minutes, then turn left side of grill off and right side to medium-low. Place loaf on left cooking grid. Close lid and grill 10 minutes, turning once. Or, alternately, heat bread with other grilled food, placing on warming rack at back of grill.

2 loaves

Blue Cheese Bread

½ cup butter or margarine, softened
¼ cup crumbled blue cheese
1 loaf (1 pound) French bread
2 tablespoons grated Parmesan cheese

Combine butter and blue cheese; blend well. Cut loaf diagonally into 1-inch slices without cutting through bottom of loaf. Spread butter mixture on slices. Spread any remaining butter mixture over top of loaf. Sprinkle with Parmesan cheese. Wrap loaf in double thickness of heavy-duty aluminum foil. Preheat grill on high for 10 minutes, then turn left side of grill off and right side to medium-low. Place loaf on left cooking grid. Close lid and grill 15 minutes, turning once. Or, alternately, heat bread with other grilled food, placing on warming rack at back of grill.

24 servings

Cheese Bread

½ cup butter or margarine, softened

1 cup (4 ounces) grated sharp Cheddar cheese

½ teaspoon Worcestershire sauce

1 loaf (1 pound) Italian bread

Combine butter, cheese, and Worcestershire in small bowl; blend well. Cut loaf diagonally into 1-inch slices without cutting through bottom of loaf. Spread cheese butter (or variation below) on slices. Wrap loaf in double thickness of heavy-duty aluminum foil. Preheat grill on high for 10 minutes, then turn left side off and right side to medium-low. Place loaf on left cooking grid. Close lid and grill 15 minutes, turning once. Or, alternately, heat bread with other grilled food, placing on warming rack at back of grill.

Variations: Cheese and Parsley: Add ½ cup chopped parsley to cheese butter. Poppy Seed: Add 2 tablespoons poppy seed to cheese butter. Sesame Seed: Add 4 to 5 tablespoons sesame seed to cheese butter. Onion: Add ¼ cup minced onion to cheese butter. Herb: Add chopped salad herbs to cheese butter.

1 loaf

Pumpernickel Italiano

½ cup butter or margarine, softened

⅓ cup grated Parmesan cheese

1 tablespoon Italian seasoning

2 tablespoons chopped parsley

1 round loaf (1 pound) pumpernickel bread

Combine butter, cheese, Italian seasoning, and parsley; blend well. Cut loaf in ½-inch slices without cutting through bottom of loaf. Spread cheese-butter mixture on every other slice. Cut lengthwise across loaf without cutting through bottom crust. Wrap loaf in double thickness of heavy-duty foil. Preheat grill on high for 10 minutes, then turn left side off and right side to low. Place loaf on left cooking grid. Close lid and bake 20 to 25 minutes, or until heated through. Or, alternately, heat bread with other grilled foods, placing loaf on warming rack at back of grill.

1 loaf

Mix and Match
Marinades

Here's a creative collection of suit-your-taste recipes that, when teamed with beef, poultry, pork, or seafood, become hand-in-glove flavor enhancers. To turn a ho-hum standby into a great grill standout, simply add one of these tasty, tenderizing marinades or smooth, savory sauces and watch that old favorite become a great new "flavorite"!

Red Wine Garlic Marinade

1 cup red wine
2 tablespoons tarragon
   vinegar

2 tablespoons vegetable oil
1 teaspoon oregano
2 cloves garlic, minced

Combine all ingredients in small bowl. Pour over beef, poultry, or shrimp in plastic bag or shallow dish. Seal bag or cover dish. Refrigerate at least 2 hours, turning occasionally. Drain, reserving marinade. Grill as desired, basting often with marinade.

1¼ cups

Tomato-Wine Marinade

¾ cup dry red wine
½ cup vegetable oil
⅓ cup chili sauce or catsup
1 tablespoon
   Worcestershire sauce

1 tablespoon lemon juice
1 tablespoon instant
   minced onion
1 teaspoon prepared
   mustard

Combine all ingredients in small bowl and blend well. Pour over beef or chicken in plastic bag or shallow dish. Seal bag or cover dish. Refrigerate at least 2 hours, turning occasionally. Drain, reserving marinade. Grill as desired, basting often with marinade.

1 cup

Marinade Italiano

1 cup Italian salad dressing	⅛ teaspoon cracked
1 small onion, chopped	peppercorns
⅛ teaspoon oregano	

Combine all ingredients in small bowl and blend well. Pour over poultry, shrimp, or less tender cuts of beef in plastic bag or shallow dish. Seal bag or cover dish. Refrigerate at least 8 hours, turning occasionally. Drain, reserving marinade. Grill as desired, basting often with marinade.

1 cup

Vinaigrette Marinade

1½ cups vegetable oil	2 teaspoons dry mustard
1½ cups wine vinegar	2 teaspoons salt
¾ cup soy sauce	1 teaspoon freshly ground
¼ cup Worcestershire sauce	pepper
⅓ cup lemon juice	2 cloves garlic, minced

Combine all ingredients in medium bowl; blend well. Pour half of marinade over chicken (or less tender cuts of beef) in plastic bag or shallow dish. Seal bag or cover dish. Refrigerate at least 4 hours, turning occasionally. Drain, reserving marinade. Grill as desired, basting often with marinade. Remaining marinade can be refrigerated for up to 6 weeks.

4⅓ cups

Beef Marinade

¾ cup dry red wine	1 tablespoon minced onion
½ cup vegetable oil	1 teaspoon rosemary
½ cup catsup	1 teaspoon salt
1 tablespoon	¼ teaspoon cracked
Worcestershire sauce	peppercorns

Combine all ingredients in small bowl and blend well. Pour over beef roast in plastic bag or shallow dish. Seal bag or cover dish. Refrigerate at least 2 hours, turning occasionally. Drain, reserving marinade. Grill roast as desired, basting often with marinade.

2 cups

Sapporo Teriyaki Marinade

⅓ cup soy sauce
2 tablespoons vegetable oil
2 tablespoons honey
¼ cup beer
1 teaspoon minced fresh
   ginger, or ¼ teaspoon
   ground ginger

½ teaspoon dry mustard
1 clove garlic, minced

Combine all ingredients in small bowl and blend well. Pour over beef, poultry, or shrimp in plastic bag or shallow dish. Seal bag or cover dish. Refrigerate at least 4 hours, turning occasionally. Drain, reserving marinade. Grill as desired, basting often with marinade.

⅔ cup

Oriental Barbecue Sauce

⅔ cup wine vinegar
½ cup pineapple juice
¼ cup soy sauce
1 teaspoon dry mustard

1 teaspoon minced fresh
   ginger, or ½ teaspoon
   ground ginger

Combine all ingredients in small bowl and blend well. Grill spareribs, chicken wings, or shrimp, basting occasionally with sauce.

1½ cups

For a surprise flavor, substitute sake or dry sherry for the vinegar.

Sour Cream and Walnut Sauce

1 container (8 ounces)
   dairy sour cream
2 to 4 tablespoons
   prepared horseradish
⅓ cup coarsely chopped
   walnuts

¼ teaspoon salt
Dash freshly ground
   pepper

Combine all ingredients in small bowl; blend well. Serve with grilled roast beef or fish.

1 cup

Orange Sauce

1 cup frozen orange juice
   concentrate, thawed
½ cup soy sauce
¼ cup sherry
1 teaspoon dry mustard

¼ teaspoon paprika
1 large clove garlic,
   minced
1 teaspoon cornstarch
⅓ cup raisins (optional)

Combine all ingredients except cornstarch and raisins in small bowl; blend well. Pour over chicken, duck, or ham in plastic bag or shallow dish. Seal bag or cover dish. Refrigerate at least 4 hours, turning occasionally. Drain, reserving marinade, and grill as desired, basting often with marinade. Stir cornstarch into reserved marinade in small saucepan. Cook over low heat, stirring constantly, until thickened. Stir in raisins, if desired. Serve hot sauce with grilled food.

1½ cups

Plum Chutney Barbecue Sauce

1 cup coarsely chopped red
   onions
1 green pepper, coarsely
   chopped
1 orange, peeled, sectioned,
   seeded, and quartered
1 large tomato, peeled,
   seeded, cored, and
   coarsely chopped

2 cloves garlic, minced
½ cup fresh lime juice
1 jar (12 ounces) plum
   preserves or jam
1 teaspoon cinnamon
½ teaspoon nutmeg
½ teaspoon salt
¼ teaspoon ginger
⅛ teaspoon cloves

Combine onions, green pepper, orange, tomato, garlic, and lime juice in medium saucepan. Bring to a boil; reduce heat. Simmer, uncovered, 45 minutes, stirring occasionally. Purée in blender or food processor. Stir in plum preserves and seasonings. Return to saucepan and simmer 15 minutes, stirring often. Serve with chicken or ribs.

3½ cups

Hot Mustard Sauce

1 cup dry mustard	1 egg yolk
1 cup vinegar	1 cup sugar
2 eggs	

Blend mustard and vinegar in small bowl. Cover and let stand at least 8 hours. Beat eggs, egg yolk, and sugar in separate small bowl until smooth. Combine mustard with egg mixture in top of double boiler. Simmer over low heat about 20 minutes, stirring constantly, until consistency of pudding. Let cool to room temperature. Use in sandwiches or as sauce for grilled meat. Refrigerate unused sauce.

2 cups

Beef Seasoning Salt

1 tablespoon onion salt	1¼ teaspoons cracked
1 tablespoon garlic powder	peppercorns
1 tablespoon paprika	

Combine all ingredients in small dish; blend well. Sprinkle on beef roast, steaks, hamburgers, or other cuts of beef just before grilling.

3½ tablespoons

Jane's Mustard Sauce

¼ cup sugar	1 cup half and half
2 tablespoons dry mustard	¼ cup vinegar
1 tablespoon all-purpose flour	2 egg yolks

Combine all ingredients in heavy saucepan or top of double boiler. Cook over low heat until slightly thickened, stirring constantly with wire whisk. Do not boil. Remove from heat and let stand until cool. Serve hot or cold with ham or beef.

1 cup

The Crowning Touch

One of the most surprising features of the gas grill is that you can even bake on it. Yes, bake! No ordinary grill can match this capability. It takes no more fuss than conventional oven baking, yet it frees you from a hot kitchen. Follow our easy instructions and you'll be turning out a wealth of pies, cakes, and fruit desserts. These more-than-welcome finales provide the crowning touch to any happy occasion.

Apple Pie

Pastry for 2-crust pie
2 pounds cooking apples, peeled, cored, and thinly sliced (5 to 6 cups)
⅔ cup sugar
1 tablespoon all-purpose flour
⅛ teaspoon salt
½ teaspoon cinnamon
¼ teaspoon nutmeg
2 tablespoons lemon juice
1 tablespoon butter or margarine

Prepare pie crust dough. Roll out bottom crust 1 inch larger than 9-inch pie plate. Fit crust into pie plate; set aside. Spread half of apples in bottom crust. Combine sugar, flour, salt, cinnamon, and nutmeg. Sprinkle half of sugar mixture and half of lemon juice over apples. Repeat for remaining apples, sugar mixture, and lemon juice. Dot with butter. Roll out remaining dough and place over filling. Seal and flute edge. Cut slits or decorative holes in top to vent steam. Preheat grill on high for 5 minutes. Turn left side of grill off and right side to medium-low. Invert a pan on left cooking grid. Place pie on inverted pan. Close lid and bake 55 to 65 minutes, or until crust is golden brown and filling is bubbly, rotating after about 30 minutes.

6 servings

Cherry Pie

Pastry for 2-crust pie

2 cans (16 ounces each) pitted sour red cherries packed in water, drained

1 cup sugar

2 tablespoons quick-cooking tapioca

⅛ teaspoon salt

½ teaspoon almond extract

1 tablespoon butter or margarine, melted

3 to 4 drops red food coloring

Prepare pie crust dough. Roll out bottom crust 1 inch larger than 9-inch pie plate. Fit crust into pie plate; set aside. Combine cherries, sugar, tapioca, salt, almond extract, butter, and food coloring in large bowl; blend well. Let stand 15 minutes. Preheat grill on medium for 10 minutes. Turn filling into pie crust. Roll out remaining dough and place over filling. Seal and flute edges. Cut slits or decorative holes in top crust to vent steam. Turn left side of grill off and right side to medium-low. Invert a pan on left cooking grid. Place pie on inverted pan. Close lid and bake 55 to 65 minutes, or until crust is golden brown and filling is thickened, rotating pie after about 40 minutes. Let stand to cool slightly before serving.

6 servings

Praline Coffee Cake

1 box (9 ounces) yellow cake mix

1 cup packed light brown sugar

1 tablespoon all-purpose flour

1 egg, lightly beaten

2 tablespoons butter

½ teaspoon vanilla

½ cup chopped pecans

Grease and flour 9-inch square baking pan; set aside. Preheat grill on medium for 10 minutes. Prepare cake mix according to package directions. Pour batter into prepared pan. Turn left side of grill off and invert a pan on left cooking grid. Place cake pan on top of inverted pan. Close lid and bake 20 minutes. Rotate pan and bake 5 minutes, or until center springs back when lightly touched. Set aside to cool. Combine brown sugar, flour, and egg in small bowl. Melt butter in skillet on right cooking grid over low heat. Stir in sugar mixture and cook 5 minutes, stirring often. Remove from grill. Stir in vanilla and pecans. Spread pecan mixture evenly over cooled coffee cake. Return cake to grill on top of inverted pan. Turn heat to medium-high and bake 8 minutes, or until topping is set. Remove coffee cake from grill and let stand until cool. Cut into squares and serve.

9 3-inch squares

Applesauce Spice Cake

2½ cups all-purpose flour
1½ teaspoons baking soda
½ teaspoon salt
½ teaspoon cinnamon
½ teaspoon cloves
½ teaspoon nutmeg
½ teaspoon allspice
2 tablespoons unsweetened cocoa

1½ cups granulated sugar
½ cup packed brown sugar
⅔ cup vegetable oil
3 eggs
1 teaspoon vanilla
2 cups applesauce
½ cup raisins (optional)
2 tablespoons powdered sugar

Grease and flour 12-cup Bundt-type pan; chill. Preheat grill on medium for 10 minutes. Combine flour, baking soda, salt, spices, and cocoa in bowl; set aside. Combine granulated and brown sugar, oil, eggs, and vanilla in large mixing bowl; beat until smooth. Alternately add flour mixture and applesauce; beat until well blended; scraping bowl often. Stir in raisins, if desired. Pour batter into prepared pan. Turn left side of grill off and invert a baking pan on left cooking grid. Place cake pan on inverted pan. Turn right side of grill to medium-low. Close lid and bake 45 to 55 minutes, or until golden. Cool in pan 10 minutes, then turn out onto wire rack to cool completely. Sprinkle with powdered sugar.

10 to 12 servings

Toasted Cake Slices with Fruit

1 frozen pound cake
(10¾ ounces), thawed
and cut in 1-inch slices
2 cups assorted fruit,
such as berries, sliced
peaches, sliced bananas,
and apricots

Sweetened whipped
cream or dairy sour
cream

Place cake slices in wire grill basket sprayed with nonstick cooking spray. Preheat grill on medium for 10 minutes, then turn left side of grill off and right side to low. Place grill basket on right cooking grid and grill, 2 to 4 minutes, or until cake is lightly toasted, turning after 1 minute. (Or, alternately, place slices directly on lightly greased cooking grid and toast, turning with long-handled spatula.) Place slices on individual serving plates; top with fruit and whipped cream.

6 to 8 servings

Patio Date Cake

1 package (8 ounces)
chopped pitted dates
1½ cups hot water
1½ teaspoons baking soda,
divided
½ cup vegetable shortening
1½ cups sugar, divided
2 eggs

½ teaspoon vanilla
1⅔ cups all-purpose
flour
½ teaspoon salt
1 package (6 ounces)
semisweet chocolate
pieces
½ cup chopped pecans

Grease and flour 8-inch square baking pan; set aside. Combine dates and water in small saucepan. Simmer until dates are soft, stirring often. Stir in 1 teaspoon baking soda; set aside. Cream shortening and 1 cup sugar in mixing bowl until smooth. Add eggs and vanilla; blend well. Stir in date mixture. Combine flour, salt, and remaining ½ teaspoon baking soda. Add to mixing bowl; blend well. Pour batter into prepared pan. Combine chocolate pieces, remaining ½ cup sugar, and nuts; sprinkle over batter. Preheat grill on medium for 10 minutes, then turn left side of grill off and invert a pan on left cooking grid. Place cake pan on inverted pan. Close lid and bake 40 minutes, rotating pan after 20 minutes, or until a wooden pick inserted in center comes out clean. Cool in pan on wire rack before serving.

16 2-inch squares

Apple Crisp

1 can (1 pound 5 ounces)
   apple pie filling
⅓ cup packed brown sugar
½ teaspoon cinnamon
¼ teaspoon nutmeg
2 tablespoons lemon juice
½ package (18½ ounces)
   yellow cake mix
   (2 cups)

½ cup butter or margarine,
   cut in thin slices
Whipped topping or
   ice cream

Pour pie filling into 9-inch baking pan. Sprinkle with brown sugar, cinnamon, nutmeg, and lemon juice. Sprinkle cake mix over apples to cover. Dot with butter slices. Preheat grill on medium for 10 minutes, then turn left side of grill off and invert a baking pan on left cooking grid. Place baking pan on inverted pan. Close lid and bake 55 to 65 minutes, or until browned and bubbly. Let stand until warm. Serve topped with whipped topping or ice cream.

6 to 8 servings

Hot Apple Slices

4 medium apples, peeled,
   cored, and sliced
2 tablespoons lemon juice
1 tablespoon brown sugar
   or honey

½ teaspoon cinnamon,
   mace, or coriander
2 tablespoons butter or
   margarine

Place apple slices in center of large sheet of heavy-duty aluminum foil. Sprinkle with lemon juice, brown sugar, and cinnamon. Dot with butter. Fold edges up and over to seal. Preheat grill on medium for 10 minutes, then turn left side of grill off and right side to low. Place packet on heated cooking grid. Close lid and grill 12 to 15 minutes, or until apples are tender. Serve with whipped topping or as accompaniment to pork.

4 servings

Iron Skillet Corn Bread

1¼ cups yellow cornmeal	2 eggs, lightly beaten
¾ cup all-purpose flour	1 cup milk
2½ teaspoons baking powder	2 tablespoons butter or
1 to 2 tablespoons sugar	margarine
½ teaspoon salt	

Preheat grill on medium for 10 minutes. Place 8-inch cast-iron skillet on right side of cooking grid. Combine cornmeal, flour, baking powder, sugar, and salt in mixing bowl. Mix eggs and milk in separate bowl. Add to dry ingredients, stirring until ingredients are just moistened. Melt butter in hot skillet on grill. Turn left side of grill off and right side to medium-low. Invert a pan on left cooking grid. Pour batter into skillet. Place skillet on inverted pan. Close lid and bake 35 minutes, or until golden brown. Cut into wedges and serve.

8 servings

Fruit Kabobs

3 cups assorted fresh or canned fruit, such as: pineapple chunks, cooked pitted prunes, peach halves, pear halves, maraschino cherries, firm bananas, cut in chunks, apricot halves	1 cup honey
	1½ tablespoons lemon juice
	½ cup butter or margarine, melted

Thread fruit onto 6 metal skewers. Blend honey and lemon juice. Brush sauce over fruit; set aside. Lightly grease cooking grid. Preheat grill on medium for 10 minutes, then turn to low. Place kabobs on cooking grid. Close lid and grill 15 to 20 minutes, or until hot, turning frequently and basting with melted butter. Watch carefully to avoid burning.

6 servings

Bran Muffins

1 cup bran cereal nuggets
1 cup milk
1 cup all-purpose flour
¼ cup sugar
½ teaspoon salt
1 tablespoon baking
   powder

1 egg, lightly beaten
2 tablespoons vegetable oil
Butter or margarine
Jam (optional)

Preheat grill on high for 5 minutes, then turn to medium. Grease 12 muffin cups. Soak cereal in milk about 5 minutes, or until milk is absorbed. Combine flour, sugar, salt, and baking powder in mixing bowl. Add egg, oil, and cereal mixture; stir until ingredients are just moistened. Fill muffin cups two-thirds full with batter. Turn left side of grill off and invert a pan on left cooking grid. Place muffin pan on top of inverted pan. Close lid and bake 17 to 20 minutes, or until golden brown, rotating pan after 8 minutes. Serve hot with butter and jam, if desired.

12 muffins

Peaches Flambé

¼ cup peach jam or
   preserves
3 tablespoons sugar
½ cup water
4 large fresh peaches,
   or. 1 can (1 pound
   12 ounces) sliced
   peaches, drained

3 tablespoons brandy
Vanilla ice cream

Preheat grill on medium for 10 minutes, then turn left side of grill off. Combine jam, sugar, and water in heavy saucepan. Place pan on cooking grid and bring to a boil. Add peaches; stir lightly to coat. Close lid and simmer about 3 to 5 minutes, or until peaches are tender. Place on warming rack until serving time. To serve, pour brandy over peaches and ignite. After flame dies, stir to blend flavors. Serve over ice cream.

6 servings

Hot 'n Sweet Grapefruit

2 grapefruits, halved,   2 teaspoons sherry
   seeded, and sectioned   ½ teaspoon nutmeg
2 teaspoons honey

Preheat grill on medium for 10 minutes, then turn left side of grill off and right side to low. Place each grapefruit half in center of large sheet of heavy-duty aluminum foil. Blend honey and sherry. Brush over grapefruit halves. Sprinkle with nutmeg. Bring edges of foil up and over to seal. Place on cooking grid. Close lid and grill 8 to 10 minutes, or until heated through. (Or, alternately, grill with other food, placing packets on warming rack and heating 15 to 20 minutes.)

2 to 4 servings

Pineapple in Foil

1 fresh pineapple, peeled,   3 to 4 tablespoons honey
   cored, and cut in   ¼ cup dark rum (optional)
   spears or rings

Place pineapple in center of large sheet of heavy-duty aluminum foil. Drizzle honey and rum, if desired, over fruit. Bring edges of foil up and over to seal. Preheat grill on medium for 10 minutes, then turn left side of grill off. Place packet on right cooking grid. Close lid and grill 8 to 10 minutes, or until heated through. (Or, alternately, grill with other food, placing packet on warming rack and heating 15 to 20 minutes.) Serve with ham or barbecued pork.

4 to 6 servings

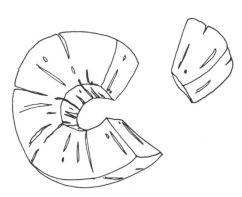

Rum-Baked Bananas

4 firm bananas, peeled
⅓ cup packed dark
    brown sugar
¼ cup dark rum

½ teaspoon cinnamon
¼ teaspoon ground cloves
3 tablespoons butter or
    margarine

Place bananas in center of a large sheet of heavy-duty aluminum foil. Combine brown sugar, rum, cinnamon, and cloves; pour over bananas. Dot with butter. Bring edges of foil up and over to seal. Preheat grill on medium for 10 minutes, then turn left side of grill off and right side to medium-low. Place packet on left cooking grid. Close lid and grill 10 minutes, or until heated through. Serve in individual dessert dishes topped with sauce from packet.

4 servings

Peaches in Foil

4 medium-size fresh
    peaches, peeled and
    sliced
1 tablespoon lemon juice

2 tablespoons brown sugar
1 teaspoon cinnamon
1 tablespoon butter or
    margarine

Place peach slices in center of large sheet of heavy-duty aluminum foil. Sprinkle with lemon juice, brown sugar, and cinnamon. Dot with butter. Fold edges of foil up and over to seal. Preheat grill on medium for 10 minutes, then turn left side of grill off and right side to low. Place packet on right cooking grid. Close lid and grill 10 to 12 minutes, or until peaches are tender. Remove peaches from packet and serve over ice cream or pound cake, or serve as accompaniment to ham or poultry.

4 servings

Grill-a-Meal

The gas grill enables the outdoor chef to take full advantage of the weather, relaxing outside while an entire meal cooks on the grill. You no longer need to keep track of the electric frypan, stovetop, and oven to set a complete award-winning meal on the table. This chapter presents a unique collection of menus, from luncheons and brunches to a full-blown picnic for a crowd. But this is just the beginning! Your own imagination will quickly provide other menus as your mood demands.

Seven-Minute Breakfast for Four

Fried Eggs	Toasted English Muffins
Honey Ham Slices	Fresh coffee

Preheat grill on medium for 5 minutes. Prepare ingredients for Fried Eggs and Honey Ham Slices; split and butter 4 English muffins. Turn heat to low. Place egg skillet and ham pan on cooking grid. Place muffins, buttered side down, on cooking grid. Close lid and grill 5 minutes. Turn muffins. Grill 2 more minutes, or until eggs are set. Serve with coffee.

Fried Eggs

4 large eggs	1 tablespoon butter or margarine

Melt butter in large skillet. Break eggs into skillet. Continue as directed above.

Honey Ham Slices

4 precooked ham slices	1 tablespoon honey
¼ cup apple juice	

Place ham slices in 8-inch pan. Pour apple juice and honey over ham. Cover with aluminum foil. Continue as directed above.

Pancake and Bacon Breakfast for Four

Saucy Fruit Kabobs
Buttermilk Blueberry
   Pancakes
Crisp Bacon Slices

Warm maple syrup
Chilled juice
Fresh coffee

Prepare ingredients for Saucy Fruit Kabobs; set aside. Preheat grill on high for 10 minutes, placing 8-inch cast-iron skillet on grill after 5 minutes to preheat. Prepare Buttermilk Blueberry Pancake batter. Pour 1 cup maple syrup into small pan; cover and set aside. Turn heat to medium-high. Place 8 to 12 slices bacon in a separate skillet on cooking grid. Heat 1 tablespoon oil in preheated skillet. Add pancake batter by quarter-cupfuls and cook 1 to 2 minutes or until bubbly. Turn and cook until browned. Remove to serving platter and cover to keep warm. Repeat with remaining batter. Place kabobs on cooking grid. (For less well browned fruit, place on sheet of aluminum foil.) Close lid and grill 8 minutes, turning once. Place syrup on warming rack during last 5 minutes to warm. Serve with chilled juice and coffee.

Saucy Fruit Kabobs

2 cups assorted fruit, such
   as pineapple chunks,
   apple wedges,
   and peach slices
¼ cup orange juice

1 tablespoon lemon juice
1 tablespoon grated
   lemon peel
¼ cup maple syrup
1 tablespoon cream sherry

Thread fruit on wooden skewers; set aside. Combine juices, lemon peel, and syrup in small saucepan and heat until warm. Remove from heat and stir in sherry. Brush sauce over kabobs. Continue as directed above.

Buttermilk Blueberry Pancakes

1 cup all-purpose flour
2 teaspoons sugar
¼ teaspoon salt
¾ teaspoon baking powder
½ teaspoon baking soda
¼ teaspoon grated
    lemon peel

1 cup buttermilk
1 egg, lightly beaten
2 tablespoons butter,
    melted
1 cup blueberries, rinsed
    and well drained

Combine dry ingredients in mixing bowl. Add buttermilk, egg, and butter; stir just until ingredients are moistened. Gently stir in blueberries. Continue as directed on page 124.

Weekend Brunch for Four

Sausage and Pineapple Kabobs	Grilled Hashed Browns
	Warm sweet rolls
Scrambled Eggs with Green Onion	Chilled juice
	Fresh coffee

Preheat grill on medium for 10 minutes. Assemble ingredients for Grilled Hashed Browns, Sausage and Pineapple Kabobs, and Scrambled Eggs with Green Onions. Wrap sweet rolls in heavy-duty aluminum foil. Place hash browns on cooking grid. Close lid and grill 10 minutes, breaking up potatoes and stirring often. Turn heat to low. Place scrambled eggs and kabobs on cooking grid. Place rolls on warming rack. Close lid and grill 5 minutes, stirring eggs often and turning kabobs once. Serve with chilled juice and coffee.

Grilled Hashed Browns

1 package (10 ounces) frozen shredded hashed brown potatoes	½ cup butter or margarine
	3 tablespoons minced onion

Melt butter in large cast-iron skillet. Add onions and cook until lightly browned. Add hashed browns to skillet and continue as directed above.

Sausage and Pineapple Kabobs

1 package (10 ounces)
brown-and-serve
sausages, cut in 1-inch
pieces
1 can (20 ounces)
pineapple chunks,
drained

2 tablespoons honey
1 teaspoon lemon juice
⅛ teaspoon celery seed

Thread sausage and pineapple pieces onto metal skewers. Combine remaining ingredients and brush sauce over kabobs. Continue as directed on page 126.

Scrambled Eggs with Green Onion

6 eggs
2 tablespoons milk
2 green onions,
thinly sliced

½ teaspoon sage
Salt
Freshly ground pepper

Combine eggs and milk in medium bowl; beat until foamy. Stir in green onions, sage, and salt and pepper to taste. Pour into greased 8-inch skillet. Continue as directed on page 126.

Patio Brunch for Six

Egg and Cheese Bake
Raspberry Streusel
Coffee Cake

Grilled Pork Sausages
Chilled fruit juice
Fresh coffee

Prepare ingredients for Egg and Cheese Bake and Raspberry Streusel; set aside. Place 12 pork sausages in 8-inch cast-iron skillet or baking dish. Preheat grill on medium for 10 minutes, then turn left side of grill off and right side to low. Place coffee cake on left cooking grid. Place Egg and Cheese Bake and sausages on right cooking grid. Close lid and bake 25 to 30 minutes, turning sausages occasionally, until eggs are set, sausages are browned, and coffee cake springs back when lightly touched in center. Serve with juice and coffee.

Egg and Cheese Bake

6 eggs, lightly beaten
1 cup (4 ounces) shredded
　　Cheddar cheese
2 tablespoons butter,
　　melted
½ cup milk

¼ teaspoon prepared
　　mustard
½ teaspoon salt
　　Dash freshly ground
　　pepper

Combine all ingredients in mixing bowl; blend well. Pour eggs into greased 9-inch baking dish. Continue as directed above.

Raspberry Streusel Coffee Cake

2 cups buttermilk baking
   mix
¼ cup sugar
1 teaspoon cinnamon,
   divided
¼ teaspoon nutmeg
1 egg

⅔ cup milk
¼ cup raspberry preserves
¼ cup all-purpose flour
¼ cup butter or margarine,
   softened
½ cup firmly packed
   brown sugar

Combine baking mix, sugar, ½ teaspoon cinnamon, and nutmeg in large mixing bowl. Add egg and milk; stir just until ingredients are moistened. Pour batter into greased 10 x 6-inch baking pan. Dot with teaspoonfuls of preserves. Combine flour, butter, brown sugar, and remaining ½ teaspoon cinnamon; blend well. Sprinkle topping over batter. Continue as directed on page 128.

Luncheon for Four

Tomato, Onion, and
Orange Salad

Ham and Cheese Puffs
Hot Cinnamon Cider

Prepare Tomato, Onion, and Orange Salad ingredients. Cover and set aside. Prepare Ham and Cheese Puff ingredients; prepare mugs for Hot Cider. Pour cider into heatproof coffee server. Preheat grill on medium for 10 minutes, then turn left side of grill off and right side to low. Place cider on right cooking grid. Place sandwiches on left cooking grid. Close lid and bake 25 to 30 minutes, or until sandwiches are golden brown. Drizzle dressing over salad and serve with sandwiches and cider.

Tomato, Onion, and Orange Salad

Bibb lettuce
¼ cup cider vinegar
½ teaspoon sugar
⅔ cup vegetable oil
2 green onions,
    thinly sliced
½ teaspoon rosemary
½ teaspoon Italian
    seasoning

½ teaspoon freshly ground
    pepper
2 tomatoes, sliced
1 large Bermuda onion,
    sliced
2 oranges, peeled, seeded,
    and sliced

Combine vinegar, sugar, oil, green onions, and seasonings in shaker bottle or bowl. Shake or blend well; set aside. Arrange lettuce on individual serving plates. Top with tomatoes, onion, and oranges. Continue as directed above.

Ham and Cheese Puffs

4 slices boiled ham,
  cut in halves
4 slices Swiss cheese,
  cut in halves
1 package (7 ounces)
  refrigerated crescent
  rolls

4 teaspoons Dijon-style
  mustard
Thinly sliced green
  onions
Crumbled crisp-cooked
  bacon
1 egg, lightly beaten

Roll out dough and cut along perforations. Spread ½ teaspoon mustard on each dough triangle. Place 2 ham and cheese halves on each of 4 triangles. Top with green onions or bacon, if desired. Top with remaining dough triangles and press edges with fork to seal. Brush with egg. Place in greased 13 × 9-inch baking dish. Continue as directed on page 130.

Hot Cinnamon Cider

1 quart apple cider
4 cinnamon sticks

4 slices lemon

Pour cider into heatproof coffee server. Prepare as directed above. Serve in individual mugs with cinnamon sticks and lemon slices.

Steak Dinner for Four

Tossed green salad
Club Steaks with
  Mushrooms and
  Onions
Acorn Squash with
  Garden Peas

Baked Potatoes
  (page 96)
Caramel Apple Dessert

Prepare ingredients for Acorn Squash with Garden Peas; set aside. Prepare potatoes according to directions on page 96; set aside. Preheat grill on medium for 10 minutes, then turn to low. Place squash and potatoes on cooking grid. Close lid and bake 30 minutes. Prepare ingredients for Club Steaks with Mushrooms and Onions. Place mushroom and onion packet on cooking grid. Close lid and grill 30 minutes. Assemble Caramel Apple Dessert; cover and set aside. Prepare your favorite tossed salad; set aside. Ten minutes before vegetables are done, place steaks on cooking grid. Turn heat to medium. Close lid and grill 5 minutes on each side, or until desired doneness. Remove steak and vegetables from grill. Fill squash with hot peas. Serve dinner. Turn left side of grill off and right side to low. Place dessert on right cooking grid. Close lid and bake 30 minutes. Remove from grill and let stand to cool slightly. Serve with ice cream topped with peanuts.

Acorn Squash with Garden Peas

2 acorn squash (about 16
    ounces each), halved
    and seeded
4 tablespoons brown sugar

4 teaspoons butter or
    margarine
2 cups hot cooked peas

Divide brown sugar and butter among squash halves. Continue as directed above. To serve, fill grilled squash with hot peas.

Club Steaks with Mushrooms and Onions

6 ounces fresh
   mushrooms, sliced
2 medium onions,
   thickly sliced
4 club steaks
   (6 ounces each)

1 clove garlic, minced
1 teaspoon dillweed
   Freshly ground pepper

Place mushrooms and onions in center of double thickness of heavy-duty aluminum foil. Sprinkle with garlic and dillweed. Fold edges of foil up and over to seal. Slash steaks at 1½-inch intervals to prevent them from curling. Sprinkle with pepper. Continue as directed on page 132.

Caramel Apple Dessert

2 large baking apples,
   peeled, cored, and cut
   into thick wedges

⅓ cup caramel sauce
   Vanilla ice cream
   Chopped peanuts

Place apple wedges in greased 8-inch baking dish. Pour caramel sauce over apples. Continue as directed on page 132. Serve with scoops of ice cream, topped with peanuts.

Chicken Dinner for Four

Barbecued Chicken
Breasts
Wild Rice and
Sausage Casserole

Cheesy Onion Bread
Fruit salad
Chocolate Nut Brownies

Assemble ingredients for Wild Rice and Sausage casserole. Cover and set aside. Prepare batter for Chocolate Nut Brownies and pour into pan. Preheat grill on medium for 10 minutes, then turn left side of grill off and right side to medium-low. Invert a pan on left cooking grid. Place baking pan on inverted pan. Close lid and bake 25 to 30 minutes. Remove from grill; turn grill off. Cool brownies in pan on wire rack. Sprinkle with powdered sugar and cut into squares. Assemble Cheesy Onion Bread. Prepare fruit salad; cover and refrigerate. Remove cooking grid from grill. Place shallow drip pan on volcanic rock on one side of grill and fill with about 1 inch water. Lightly grease cooking grid over drip pan. Preheat grill on high for 10 minutes. (Refill drip pan if needed.) Prepare ingredients for Barbecued Chicken Breasts. Turn right side of grill to medium and left side to low. Place chicken breasts, skin side down, on right cooking grid. Place casserole opposite chicken over low heat. Close lid and grill chicken 20 to 30 minutes, or until tender, turning occasionally and basting with sauce. Stir rice after 10 minutes, then place bread next to casserole. Grill bread 5 to 8 minutes or until cheese is melted; open package and grill 3 to 5 minutes longer.

Wild Rice and Sausage Casserole

1 package (6 ounces) long
  grain and wild rice mix,
  cooked according to
  package directions
¼ pound ground pork
  sausage, cooked and
  drained

½ cup chopped onion
½ cup chopped celery
¼ cup chopped parsley
1 can (8 ounces) sliced
  water chestnuts,
  drained

Combine all ingredients in 2-quart casserole; stir lightly to blend. Continue as directed above.

Chocolate Nut Brownies

½ cup butter or margarine
2 squares (1 ounce each)
  unsweetened baking
  chocolate
1 cup sugar

¾ cup all-purpose flour
1½ teaspoons baking powder
¼ teaspoon salt
2 eggs, lightly beaten
1 teaspoon vanilla

Grease 9-inch square baking pan. Melt butter and chocolate in medium saucepan over low heat, stirring until smooth. Add sugar, flour, baking powder, and salt; blend well. Add eggs and vanilla; blend well. Pour batter into prepared pan. Bake as directed on page 134.

Cheesy Onion Bread

1 loaf (1 pound) Italian
  or sourdough bread
1 package (3 ounces)
  cream cheese, softened
1 cup (4 ounces) shredded
  mozzarella cheese
¼ cup thinly sliced
  green onions

1 teaspoon Worcestershire
  sauce
2 tablespoons butter or
  margarine,
  softened
½ teaspoon garlic powder

Cut loaf diagonally into 1-inch slices without cutting through bottom of loaf. Combine remaining ingredients; blend well. Spread cheese mixture on slices. Spread any remaining cheese mixture over top of loaf. Wrap loaf in double thickness of heavy-duty aluminum foil. Grill as directed on page 134.

Barbecued Chicken Breasts

4 boneless chicken breasts
  (8 ounces each)

½ cup bottled barbecue
  sauce or Plum Chutney
  Barbecue Sauce
  (page 110)

Rinse chicken breasts and pat dry. Brush lightly with barbecue sauce, reserving extra for basting. Continue as directed on page 134.

Picnic for Twelve

Grilled Hamburgers and
Bratwurst
Picnic Baked Beans
Potato Salad

Condiments
Pineapple Cake
Chilled beverages

Prepare Pineapple Cake batter and pour into pan. Preheat grill on medium for 10 minutes, then turn left side of grill off and right side to medium-low. Invert a pan on left cooking grid. Place baking pan on inverted pan. Close lid and bake 45 to 55 minutes, or until golden brown, rotating after 20 minutes. Remove cake from grill. Cool in pan on wire rack. Frost with Cream Cheese Frosting. Prepare Potato Salad; cover and refrigerate. Prepare Picnic Baked Beans ingredients. Turn heat to medium. Place beans on cooking grid. Close lid and grill 45 minutes, stirring occasionally. While beans are cooking, prepare ingredients for Grilled Hamburgers and Bratwurst. After beans have cooked 30 minutes, place hamburgers on cooking grid. Close lid and grill 5 minutes. Add bratwurst. Close lid and grill 10 to 14 minutes, or until desired doneness, turning hamburgers once and bratwurst occasionally. Place buns, cut side down, on warming rack 5 minutes before removing bratwurst and hamburgers from grill. Serve in buns with desired condiments.

Pineapple Cake

2 cups all-purpose flour
2 cups sugar
1 teaspoon baking soda
½ teaspoon nutmeg

2 eggs
1 can (20 ounces) crushed
  pineapple, undrained
1 cup chopped pecans

Grease 13 × 9-inch baking pan. Combine all ingredients in mixing bowl; blend well. Pour batter into prepared pan. Bake as directed above. Frost with Cream Cheese Frosting.

Cream Cheese Frosting

1 package (8 ounces)
  cream cheese,
  softened

1⅓ cups powdered sugar
1 tablespoon half and half
1 teaspoon vanilla

Combine all ingredients in small mixing bowl; beat until smooth.

Picnic Baked Beans

6 slices bacon, chopped
1 cup chopped onions
4 cans (16 ounces each)
   Great Northern beans,
   drained
2 cans (8 ounces each)
   tomato sauce
½ cup molasses

¼ cup chili sauce
2 tablespoons prepared
   mustard
2 teaspoons
   Worcestershire sauce
1 teaspoon hot pepper
   sauce

Cook bacon in skillet until crisp. Remove from pan with slotted spoon and drain on paper towels. Add onion to bacon drippings; cook, stirring frequently, until onion is tender. Drain off fat. Combine remaining ingredients in 2-quart casserole. Add onion and bacon and blend well. Continue as directed on page 136.

12 servings

Grilled Hamburgers and Bratwurst

3 pounds lean ground beef
1 egg, lightly beaten
12 precooked bratwurst

12 hamburger buns
12 bratwurst buns

Break up beef and lightly work in egg with fingers. If desired, add other flavoring ingredients from list for Made-to-Order Hamburgers (page 46). Slit or puncture bratwurst casings to prevent bursting. Split hamburger and bratwurst buns; butter lightly if desired. Continue as directed on page 136.

INDEX